What's Tarot Got To Do With It?

The Fool's Path to Enlightenment

By Jim Larsen

With foreword by Dr. James Wanless

Illustrations from The Fool's Path Tarot by Jim Larsen

Printed in the United States of America

First Printing, 2014

ISBN 978-0-9912920-0-4

Dedication
The Fool in me recognizes and honors the Fool in you

Contents

Acknowledgments

I wish thank the many people I have done tarot card readings for in all the places in the world I have done my readings. With each reading comes new insights and knowings into the truth of each archetype which will always be invaluably beneficial in articulating my personal interpretations.

I also wish to thank James Wanless who's tarot guidance and friendship has been instrumental in my waking up, and whose Voyager Tarot Fool Child card continues to be my personal Jesus.

And a big thank you to the ever rotating, ever changing cast of characters at Kalani Oceanside Retreat on The Big Island of Hawaii who have become as much my ohana (family) as my own blood relatives. Without such fellow truth seekers, I would never have had the conversations that prompted me to look for personal answers. Had I never sought personal answers, I probably would have stayed content as a government contractor riding the metro to work in the city where my cubicle would be waiting for me everyday for my whole life, never to become the roving student of life I turned into. Wow. Dodged that bullet!

Foreword

Jim Larsen's "Dedication" in "What's Tarot Got To Do With It?" says it all, "The Fool in me recognizes and honors the Fool in you." Indeed, and rightly so! Read the lengthy and tremendously insightful writing on the tarot's Fool Card and you will understand the invaluable and incalculable importance of embodying the Fool in your own life. As the Fool marches to his or her own's drum and heartbeat of the spirit, you are authentic, living your life your way, which is the way to "personal enlightenment" as described in this book.

Larsen finishes his own life voyage through the tarot as he writes, "Do what is best for your journey! Not somebody else's journey. Their journey is their journey. Your journey is your journey and that is what you are responsible for. Remember that. If you do this, you are on the path- the right path. You are living an Enlightened Life, and as such you are an inspiration for others. Keep going."

"What's Tarot Got To Do With It?" is Jim Larsen's own Fool's journey. Check out his "crazy" collage art for a complete deck of cards. They are nothing like you've seen before, as befits the true revolutionary, unconventional Fool's way of life. This book is a wonderful model for everyone to follow, in their own way, of course. I would love to see tarot enthusiasts make their own deck. By doing this process, you find your own way, your own symbols, your own style, your own road map – yourself.

This is a brave work. It takes great courage and trust in oneself to make some "silly" looking cards. Without breaking the taboo of silliness, one cannot be a true Fool, a genuine individual. The book is not looking for your agreement, but with your respect for an original creation. There's a lot that everyone can learn from this.

Part of the originality of this approach to the venerable tarot is the innovative way that the so-called "Minor Arcana" cards have been formulated. Rather than a rehash of the old, traditional tarot, Larsen re-visions the meaning of each suit – from Swords to Speculation, from Wands to Passions, from Cups to Desires, and from Pentacles to Creations. How refreshing! And how interesting and surprising are the Cards.

Additionally, this book's creative contribution to the field of tarot is seen in the treatment of the classic Royalty Cards. They have been transformed into Students, Champions, Mothers and Fathers. I especially appreciate Jim Larsen's "Fool-Child" way of life through his description of the Student of Passion, "Never be afraid to try something new. Always seek that next new thing to be fascinated by. The world is filled with "Wows!" Always be on the lookout for the next one."

I sum up this "crazy wisdom," novel tarot road map of life by one word, Wow!

– Dr. James Wanless, Creator of Voyager Tarot, Sustain Yourself Cards, and Author of Way of the Great Oracle, Intuition@Work, and Sustainable Life: The New Success

Introduction

The average tarot deck contains seventy eight cards with pictures on them. What you do with these cards and what meaning you attach to them is entirely up to you. It is a popular thing to use these cards as "fortune telling." That is to say, to divine what your future will be. There is of course, nothing wrong with that. Who hasn't sought an answer to what lies ahead at one point or another? But if that is all tarot is to you, you are missing out on a vast resource of inner reflection.

Above and beyond fortune telling, tarot is for communication with the divine and with your higher self. More than that though, it is a means to communicate with your inner self. You can ask the divine and your higher self "What is important to know?" And through tarot, an answer will come. You can ask yourself, "What is really going on with me right now?" And through tarot, an answer will come. You can ask, "What is the true content of my heart?" Tarot will guide you to an answer. You can ask, "What direction should I be headed right now?" Tarot will act as a compass pointing you in the right direction. To treat tarot as simple "fortune telling" is to severely limit its true power.

Tarot will help you understand how we all- each and every one of us live the archetypes of the universe. It will illuminate how we everyday tap into the energy and the power of these archetypes. Tarot is a blueprint of our soul and a map of our spiritual journey, and not merely cards to be read or pictures to be looked at.

This book takes a spiritual approach to tarot. It will help you understand yourself now in the context of where you have been to catch a glimpse of where you are headed. This is beyond simple "Fortune Telling." This book is about the wisdom of the cards. Each card is a piece of the puzzle of who you are. To understand the cards is to master humanity and to live fully.

The answers and the wisdom of this book are not absolute. They won't be until you attach your own understanding to them. How do the words here resonate with you? Honor that. Do you see something completely different in the cards than what is presented here? Honor that as well.

Tarot is not about concrete and definitive answers. Tarot is about interpretation and gut wisdom. What does each card say to you? That is the meaning of the card. Use this book to guide you on your tarot journey, but do not consider it as gospel truth. Use this book as a jumping off point to develop your own intuition and knowings.

Through tarot, you will discover your truth. What you see in each card as they apply to yourself and to others is what define you as an earthly being in many ways. With each card being a piece of whom we each are, how could it not? Tarot is universal, yet personal. How do you view yourself as an individual in the context of the universal allness? This book is here to help you find this answer.

Tarot and Enlightenment

What is the point of it all anyway? Why are we here? Why do we get born? What is the meaning and the purpose of our life? Is there a grand scheme to it all? A grand purpose? How do our lives fit into the ultimate meaning of the universe? In what way do we fit into the context of the whole of everything that is- the All that is the Allness of All? Why even have humans on the planet in the first place?

A great and true purpose of our life, our presence in human form upon the earth is to learn lessons. Our spirits strive to attain perfection. Perfection comes from mastering what it means to be in human form. In human form, we experience joy, pain, happiness, sorrow, worry, jealousy, hardship, ease, highs, lows, ups, downs, empathy, anger, contentment, bliss, peace, rage… the list goes on. Each of these things, when mastered, contributes to the strength of our spirit.

In human form, we are given multiple opportunities to experience each emotion and each human feeling. To learn from these emotions and feelings, we must face them. They are not all fun, and they are not all pleasant. Some of them make us want to run away as far as we can and hide and never deal with them. You can do that if you want, for you do have free will, but it would be a mistake. We lose valuable opportunities for our personal enlightenment when we do.

By experiencing each feeling and each emotion, we absorb the strength of each, even the unpleasant ones. When these feelings feel good, such as joy, happiness, and love, it is pleasant to absorb them. The reality of living is though, they do not all feel good. Much of what we feel is downright undesirable, such as anger, sadness, and frustration. These feelings are not designed to be the enemy, to cause us strife and misery. No, they are a part of the sum total of who we are.

To be complete, we must integrate even that which makes us the most uncomfortable. We must master each feeling and each emotion by facing them head on and standing strong in the face of them. To take them in,

1

process them, understand where they come from and what they are telling us is to master even the hardest emotion to face. So we design a life for ourselves where opportunities are given to face that which we still must face and integrate that which we still must integrate.

Three Assumptions

There are three assumptions that this book makes. Number one is that we each have incarnated on the earth numerous times, and that each time we have worked towards becoming a little more perfect. You are in your present incarnation to build upon what you have been working on for all your incarnations- the perfection of your spirit.

Maybe you have a sense of what you need to work on, and maybe you don't. Conscious awareness is unimportant. Just live your life the best you can, and in so doing, your purpose is being fulfilled. Are you happy doing what you are doing? Do things feel right? Yes? You are on the right track. Does something feel off? Not quite right? Completely wrong? Pay attention to this feeling. What can you do to feel more right?

The second assumption is that prior to your birth this lifetime, you had a planning session with a team of divine helpers to create a life that will facilitate your spiritual growth. That is to say, you in spirit form assessed and analyzed your current spiritual progress to determine what more you need to experience in order to learn the lessons yet to learn. From this, a "Life Plan" was created to present to you chances for growth while on the earth.

That is not to say that every action and every movement you make is preplanned. No. It is to say the opportunities to learn these lessons will be presented. The choice is yours in human form to act on them. If you do choose to act on them, great! Check those experiences off the list and move on to the next. If you choose not to, well, that's okay. There are no penalties. Another opportunity will just have to be created for you to learn this lesson, that's all.

The third assumption is that while in human form on the earth, you are not alone. You have a tremendous team of spirit guides, angels, ascended masters, and other such divine helpers watching over you and guiding you on your journey through this lifetime. They know your Life Plan. They know what you need to experience for your own growth. They see a much bigger picture for your life than your limited, human perspective can imagine. They are ever nudging you in the right direction.

Now mind you, they will only nudge you. Any decisions to be made are up to you to make. They honor your free will even when it pains them. They have such a grand view of what your life is and what it can be that they want to shout "Do this!" Or, "Don't do that!" Because they know what is best. But they patiently and diligently nudge you, creating synchronicities that allow you to get the most out of life and to reach your own Personal Enlightenment.

Maybe they actually will shout to you. Have you ever heard them? Have you heard your name in an in between moment, called as if from far away? Have you inexplicably awoken to the sound of bells ringing? Did you pay attention to them?

Personal Enlightenment

The path to Enlightenment is personal. This is not "Enlightenment" as a grand idea that only special people can achieve, but rather the accumulation of efforts of each individual person in shedding the extra weight and baggage they have picked up over the course of their lifetime and being made light. It is about accepting, integrating, and understanding the darkness and shadows that we each have as part of our being. It is about the path to personal understanding and acceptance.

"Personal Enlightenment" means the achievement of what you set out to learn and accomplish this lifetime. It means to get out of your own way and allow understanding to enter. Whatever the lessons are, whatever emotions and feelings you incarnated to master, whatever personal status you are here to obtain, it means you have been successful in it. Your spirit is that much stronger. You are that much more powerful. You have awakened. You heard the calls to action, and you acted on them. You did not settle for complacency, but rather chose to follow your gut and the voices of the divine even when none of it made any logical sense.

Now your energy can be devoted to further growth and spiritual advancement. You do not need to go back and repeat the lessons of this lifetime again. Sure, they will come up again; both in this lifetime and future incarnations, but you will handle them with much greater ease. Strength amassed is never lost or squandered. It will forever be a part of the being you are and all you will ever be. New lessons and opportunities can be devised for future incarnations. With this lifetime's lessons mastered, you can now go on to master more; ever inching your way to your "Grand Enlightenment" of mastering all there is to master.

It also means you are an inspiration upon the earth. People will sense in you a certain power. You will shine forth a radiance of confidence and knowingness that others will want to emulate. Help these people along the path of their own life. Share your wisdom and your knowledge. It can only help them to hear their own divine guidance and to follow the trail of synchronicities their own divine team is laying out for them.

Remember, the lesson one person may have set out to learn may have long since been mastered by another. Someone who has mastered one lesson may look at somebody who is working on that lesson for their self and ask "What is wrong with that person?" Not appreciating the effort they are putting into getting through this to be a better person.

What they should realize is that they themselves are learning lessons all their own. Perhaps these lessons are not as obvious problems such as drug addiction or alcoholism, but they are indeed here for something. Perhaps the lesson they are working on is to learn compassion or understanding for others.

What's Tarot got to do with it?

What does Tarot have to do with any of this? A lot. Consider Tarot to be a blueprint of the soul and a road map of your personal journey. Each card, each archetype, represents a piece of the human soul. We are each spirits on the earth encased in human form. As such, we share certain commonalities. There are aspects of our spiritual being and our earthly being that are universal to us all. Therefore, each can be given a name, and each can be identified. Tarot does this. Tarot both names and identifies the multitude of our shared spiritual and earthly aspects of living.

"Arcana" means "secrets" and "mysteries." Each Tarot card falls into one of two arcana's. One is the mystery of the major arcana, and the other is the mystery of the minor arcana. These are the secrets and the mysteries of life. The major arcana represent the spiritual side of our life. This is the blueprint of our soul. This is what is common and shared among us in the spiritual sense. The minor arcana represent our earthly form. This is what it means to have a shared human experience. It tells us where we are and where we are headed. In this way, it is a road map of our personal journey.

To consider where you are on your path to your Personal Enlightenment, consider what each card has to tell you, and how this archetype manifests itself within you. Meditate on the message of each card, and look within to find it. If it is easy to find, this means you have done well in mastering its lesson. If you must dig and search for it, that means this is an aspect of yourself that you are still working on. Let each archetype speak to you. Listen carefully to the messages they have. Meditate and hear. These are pieces of your soul talking. Nothing they say is arbitrary.

Meditating on the cards

When meditating on a tarot card, choose one or more qualities that the card represents to you, be it a sense of compassion, a sense of power, a sense of strength, a sense of leadership, a sense of adventure, a sense of nurturing, a sense of abundance, a sense of magic, a sense of intuition, whatever it may be. Now imagine the strongest eminence of that quality. This is personal. This is what it means to you. It doesn't have to be what it means to your spouse, partner, coworker, teacher, sibling, child, taxi driver, produce clerk, pastor, parents or anybody. What's important is what it means to you. You don't have to impress anybody with your answer. You don't even have to tell anybody if you don't want to. This is your personal meaning.

Not sure what it means to you? Wondering how to figure it out? Do this. Look at the card. What about this card makes the strongest impression on you? Is it a particular image? Is it the color scheme? Is there a look on a face in the card that stirs you in some way? Focus on this. Allow yourself to be drawn into the world of the card. Based on what you see, what do you want to do?

Do your best to allow any and all thoughts not related to the card to dissipate. Focus only on the impression the card makes on you. What actions does this impression move you to do? Ask yourself, why? Why does the card make you feel this way? Are you motivated? Repulsed? What do you want to do right now based on this card? What real world action? What imagined action where there are no limits and no repercussions? Play with this idea. Become unlimited. See yourself doing this thing and feeling good about yourself for having the power to do it. This is the power that the card has for you.

Perhaps there is a word on the card that makes an impression on you. Maybe the name of the archetype itself is powerful to you. Maybe you are considering the Emperor card, and the word "Emperor" has strong connotations to you. What does it mean to be an Emperor? What qualities does an Emperor have? Is there an example in your life of somebody you feel exemplifies the Emperor archetype? A father? A boss? A president, king, manager, supervisor? Do you see these qualities in you? Would you like to? Imagine yourself powerful, looked up to, and respected. This is your Emperor empowerment. This is how the Emperor quality is alive within you.

Let's take the Star Card as another example. Perhaps you like to sing. What does it mean to you to be a great singer? The strongest eminence of this might then be to sing with all the power and talent of Elvis Presley. Or Elvis Costello. Or Elton John. Or Lady Gaga. Or Momma Cass. Or Loretta Lynn. It is up to you. What does a perfect performance mean to you?

Who (or what) captures this idealization to you? This doesn't have to be a famous person. This could be your brother who sings around the house. It could be the person in the next cubical at work who whiles away the hours with a tune. Simply ask yourself what it means to sing perfectly. Hold this in your heart. Keep it in the center of your mind's eye. Picture this perfect performance in your mind, now shift it to yourself. See yourself giving this perfect performance. Feel it in your heart.

From your heart, let it radiate outward. As it radiates outward, it creates a powerful energy field that draws more and more of this eminence to you. Now, how can you not give the perfect performance, in time? How can you not be as successful as you want to be? Try this with everything. There are no limits.

Perhaps you wish to draw abundance into your life. Maybe you feel as though something important is lacking in your life and you want to fill that gap. The Fortune card is a good meditation focus. What does fortune mean to you? Does it mean having all you want, all you desire, and all you crave? Or does it mean having simply all you need? Is there a specific something you are trying to draw more of? Is it money? Is it success in your chosen field? Would a writer's contract fill you with a sense of abundance? Would a large haul of fish in your net give you a sense of abundance? Whatever abundance means to you, visualize it. Feel it in your heart. Fill your heart with the sensation of it until it is full from it. Let it spill over. Visualize your heart as a bathtub that is overflowing with the waters of your dreams. Let this dream fill the entirety of you.

If financial security is what you are wishing for, imagine a warehouse. This is your warehouse. Only you have the combination that opens the door. Open the door and be staggered with awe at the spectacle before you. As you open the door, it is so filled with wealth, be it dollars or francs, or euros, or Chinese RMBs, whatever it is to you. Maybe gold. Maybe diamonds. Whatever it is, see it spilling out the door because it is so full. See pile after pile, mound after mound of this vast fortune. It is all for you to do with as you please.

Hold onto the awe of this. Feel the power that this is for you. Let it emanate from you. Let it shine forth. Let it be so powerful that how could it not come to you now? Feel it so much that it is real for you. Now, go to a mound and scoop a handful and stuff it in your pocket. This in itself will be plenty for you. You can pay your bills, you can take your vacation, you can buy that house or car with just what's in your pocket. And when you need more, well, you have the combination to your warehouse so you can come back for more.

Remember, each and every card in a Tarot deck represents personal power. Find your power in the cards. Meditate on the cards to find how their power is alive inside of you and how you can tap into this power whenever you desire to. Before long, you will be living the power of each card without even thinking about it. It is just who you are. Simple as that.

The Major Arcana

The major arcana represents a blueprint of the human spirit. Here all the elements of what it means to be present in spirit form are laid out, but how is it all put together? What elements are stronger than others? What pieces dominate? Which pieces need strengthening? Which can you identify within yourself? Which are hidden? Which one or ones do you most identify with? Which one or ones seem foreign and distant from who you are?

The simple truth is, each and every card of the major arcana is a piece of who we are. The question becomes, how well do we embody each one? The answer comes down to one simple concept: awareness. Being aware of each archetype allows for the embodiment of each. To embody each archetype is to harness the power of each. To harness the power of each is to be fully actuated.

Think of the actualization of each archetype as a pursuit for this lifetime. You may not become a "master" of each, but the attempt to live up to the greatest potential of each will certainly strengthen your spirit. The more you embody the strength of each archetype, the more enlightened you become.

Take time to meditate on each of the major arcana cards. As you read about each one, consider how each is alive inside of you. Just how alive is it? Each is important to the being of the fullest person you can be. This is your spirit. Each archetype is a piece of the puzzle of who you are. Does it seem that some pieces are missing? Meditate on the cards to find these missing pieces. Does it seem you have all the pieces, but don't know how they fit together? Hold them in your heart until the pieces around them fill in and it makes more sense to you where they belong.

Take the archetypes one at a time. Meditate on each in their own time until you understand them as best you can for yourself. When you understand one at a time, the picture of how they fit together comes clear and the picture of who you are sharpens.

This picture is the truth of who you are. It is your personal truth. It represents your strengths, your weaknesses, your desires, your repulsions, and the overall goal of your Life Plan. Who are you and who do you want to be? Let the cards of the major arcana lead you in the direction of these answers.

Finding your truth will assist another and another and another and another to find theirs. Every one truth is a piece to a much bigger picture. The picture of yours, the puzzle you put together is but one piece of a much larger truth. Once all these truths are put together, what picture does it reveal? A picture of the greatness of the universe.

The Fool

0

Key Words

New Beginning
Leap of Faith
Trust
Courage
Perseverance

*The Fool maintains a soft
and flexible mind.*

We see the Fool as he embarks on his journey. He leaves behind the comfort, warmth, and familiarity of family and home to embrace the unknown. What will he find on his quest? How will he change? What will he become?

On his back, he carries all he needs. In his hand is a sponge to soak up the wisdom and the knowledge that will present itself to him. What will he do with this wisdom and knowledge? Will he save it save it in his containers to access later, or will he squander it and let it dry up?

The Fool's mind is soft and flexible. He is not rigid in his thinking and he is open to a wide variety of options and opportunities. By being unrigid, he has access to wisdom of the universe. He puts up no blocks to this divine guidance.

A Fool is one who has set out on a quest to understand who they are. They are following the trail of synchronicities to the answers that have meaning to them. The journey of any Fool is a journey to one's perfect self, and each will be different than the journey of all others because we all start from different points with a different set of understandings and knowings about who we are and what we seek.

This journey is to Enlightenment- Personal Enlightenment, for Enlightenment is a personal thing. We are One, but we are different aspects of One. Your journey will strengthen the aspect that you represent. My journey will do that for me. It's all about awakening to our unique purpose on the planet, or realizing that yes, we each do have a unique purpose.

For what reason did you incarnate at this time? Maybe you have an answer to that, and maybe you don't. Exact answers are meaningless. What matters is that you realize that somewhere in the middle of all you do, all you think, and all you believe; you are achieving your purpose.

How do you know you are achieving your purpose? You know this through the sensation of happiness and bliss. When you are on the right track, things just feel right. Life becomes easier. The struggles fall away and you feel good about what we are doing.

When you are not on the right track, you experience frustration. It seems that you constantly repeat the same struggle over and over again. This is because you are for a fact experiencing the same struggle over and over again, and will until you accept that you are on the wrong path. This is often a difficult and painful realization, so much so that your mind may reject it. Eventually though, your mind must face this if true happiness is to be realized.

It is more than happiness that is experienced upon awakening to your purpose. It is outright bliss. Complete contentment. It is up to us each of as individuals to make it happen, and when we each do, the human race is that much closer to its next step in evolution- a state of awakened individuals, each living their purpose.

This journey begins at Zero and concludes at Zero- a complete circle. From asking questions about your life, your purpose, to finding the answers.

How large will the circumference of this circle be? How long will it take you to go all the way around? What knowings, wisdom, and knowledge will you pick up along the way? What can you share with others that will help them on their journey?

A Fool's journey is a conscious journey. As a Fool you are a fearless explorer of the human condition. You understand that nothing is for nothing, and everything has its purpose. You are aware that you are never alone and that everything and everybody you encounter has their purpose, whether you understand their purpose or not. You see the value of all and seek the lessons that all encounters provide.

You trust your instincts even when there is no logical reason to. You know that the wisdom supplied by divine sources is far wiser than anything your mind will conjure. To embrace the Fool within is to become truly wise. This will put you for sure and certain on the path to enlightenment.

Like attracts like. Remember this. Light will attract light. To reveal your light, you must shed the ego and peel away the masks and layers of social conditioning that have entrapped it. While the mind is in control, this shedding will never occur. Only when the ego surrenders to the spirit will this happen. As a Fool, you are adept at letting go of the ego and peeling away the layers of social conditioning to reveal your light.

This light illuminates the truth of who you really are, not the truth of who you believe yourself to be. These are two very different truths. The truth of who you are is the you that is you that perhaps you have forgotten about. This is the you that is privy to all the wisdom of the universe. This is the you that has encoded in its very core the blueprint of the life you designed for yourself. This is the you that has etched in it, the map of the journey you chose for this lifetime . This is the you that understands without question what is in your highest and greatest good.

Consider this light that is within you as a spark. Give this spark any word you find suitable for it- spirit, light, essence. The word you use is unimportant. This is your divinity- the you that is you and always has been. This is the real you. The core you.

The truth of who you believe yourself to be, however, is the you that society

13

has created. This is the mask you wear to be what others expect you to be. This is the you that has earthly responsibilities. This is the you that gets a job, pays bills, and competes with his neighbor to have the best car. This is the you that places importance on the outcome of the Super Bowl year after year and subjugates yourself to the whims of the marketers and other such masters of manipulation. This is the you that gets married, has children, picks a favorite genre of music and sticks to that station on the radio. This is the you that dutifully watches your favorite TV shows every week and will gladly pay for a digital recorder to make sure not to miss an episode.

This is the you that gets the most attention because it has the dominate personality. This is the you that you are used to being. This is the you that you and others are comfortable with. This is the you that is nice and cozy in its comfort zone where the rules of living are so neatly printed out and easy to understand. This is the you that lulled itself into a sense of complacency. This is the you that doesn't want to rock the boat and disturb the notions it has created about its own existence. This is the you that your mind has created, severely influenced by self-judgment and marred projections.

But is it the real you? Or do you have a sense that there is more to life? More to yourself? Does it not seem that something somewhere is missing? Does it feel like something somewhere is calling out to you, wanting you to know about it, to acknowledge it? There is. It is that core you.

But if this core you is so important, why doesn't it stay on the forefront of your awareness? Why is it so easily pushed aside and forgotten? What happens to it? The answer is easy. We create cinder blocks with our thoughts that imprison it so we don't have to be bothered by it. Out of sight, out of mind.

This core self is the speaker of truth. How often are we truly ready for the truth though? Our minds and our ego have its own idea about what the truth is. When this is contrary to what our core being is telling us, we tend to ignore it. We shut it away. We tell ourselves that it can't be telling us what is right, because it is simply too outrageous. We deny our truth, and each denial becomes a cinder-block. Each misguided expectation, limiting belief, rigid thought, repeated pattern and simple misconception about what it means to be alive on the planet is a cinder-block; firmly cemented by fear, worry, disappointment and sadness.

Fear cements these cinder-blocks- fear that if we surrender to anything beyond our mind or the faith society tells us to have, that our life will fall apart. How can the spirit compete with this? It must scream to be heard. Even then, it can only hope to be acknowledged. Cinder-block by cinder-block, we wall our core self in until we forget our light is there. Our core being shut securely away, the ego now has no competition. There is nothing to challenge it, nothing to question it.

Imprisoned as it may be, our inner light is ever shining and ever patient. You may have forgotten that it is there, but it has not forgotten you. It will call out. It will send you messages. You will hear them in your dreams, in your quiet moments, during times of unexpected clarity and moments of causeless joy.

Perhaps you will hear it call your name. This may sound faint and far away, or it may be as loud as can be. However you experience it, trust it and appreciate it. You will hear it in your inspirations and your sudden knowings. It will always try to get your attention. It will always be calling out. It will find you in your meditations.

There is also a you that is outside of you. It wants to enter your heart to connect with that inner you. This is your higher self- the ultimate you, the uber you. The two ultimate, divine yous, the one within and the one beyond- they want to unite. They want to connect and share the wisdom that each has amassed so that each can grow and benefit from it. This wisdom, when combined creates a divine synergy that ripples throughout the cosmos, being picked up and shared by countless sentient beings.

What stops these two divine yous from connecting? You do. Your ego does. Your mind imposes limits on what you can accomplish and expect. Your mind, which needs to control everything to the point where your spirit doesn't have a chance to be heard over the noise it makes or be seen through the clutter it litters your inner landscape with.

The time will come though, when your core light will be contained no longer. This light is meant to fill the entirety of your being, not remain a pea-sized second thought buried somewhere in your consciousness. It is meant to expand beyond the limits of your physicality. Just as the essence of a fire is felt beyond the flame, so too is your spirit meant to be felt beyond your physicality.

Your journey on a spiritual path begins when the you that is you awakens. This is when the cement begins to crumble and the cinder-blocks fall away. Perhaps the core you finally speaks loudly enough to get your attention and you just know- your intuition kicks in and you are aware that it is time for crucial changes in your life. Or maybe something external triggers an awakening in you.

Sometimes it happens that you experience some traumatic event- injury, divorce, loss of a loved one, a drastic reduction in financial stability, and without notice you are plunged into an entirely different set of circumstances where the world your ego created for you suddenly makes no sense anymore. What do you have left now that what you understand is gone? You search your ego for an answer, but it is simply not providing one. Now you need something new to make sense to you. What else is there?

Your inner light will crack the cement binding the cinder-blocks, and it will shine outward. The outer you likewise, will call to you. It will call to you with an entire chorus of guides, guardian angels, and ascended masters all wanting you to recognize the truth of the being that is you. They want to help you live the fullest life you can live on the earth. It is their job to help, and they want to do their job to the fullest. With the cement holding this spark that is the true you now cracked and your light making its way through, you become aware of the secrets of the universe. The wisdom of that inner light becomes common knowledge, and your divine team becomes your constant companion.

This puts you on an entirely new and different path. No longer holding onto previous thoughts and beliefs, you are free to explore an entirely new plateau. This path is not pre-scribed. It is a journey that has not been written yet. This is a path of personal understandings and discoveries. This is a path without expectations, only discoveries. This is the path of the Fool, and it is blazed by the Fool himself.

To the uninitiated eye, that is to say, to one who has not yet awakened to their own divinity, the actions of a Fool may seem ridiculous. This is because they do not yet have a basis of comparison in their own experiences. They are still playing it safe. They are not yet willing to let go and follow pure faith. They see a Fool doing what, for all intents and purposes, seems crazy and it confuses them.

As an example, a Fool may know that in order to achieve their highest and best good, they need to quit their job and move to Hawaii. The uninitiated may watch this happen and say, "How can you do that? How can you give up your security for uncertainty and just go like that?"

The Fool may have a concrete answer for this, or not. In his heart of hearts, he knows he is being led to the best place for him to be to do the best things for him to be doing. So he does it. Simple as that. Does he need permission and validation from the uninitiated? Of course not. Even if these uninitiated masses may judge him, calling him an idiot behind his back, he will follow his own callings.

Of course, those uninitiated calling the Fool an idiot are way, way off. The Fool is anything but an idiot. No, a true Fool and a genuine idiot have nothing in common. The difference between a Fool and an idiot is that the Fool will take a leap of faith and assume the risk of failure without ego. An idiot, however, will take a leap of faith, anchored to his ego like an albatross around his neck. He sees in his mind only one viable outcome- the outcome he has pre-scribed for himself. He is simply caught up in the traps of the ego- that bit of being that is unable to surrender to the natural flow of what is and what was always meant to be.

If this outcome does not come to be, the Idiot will likely deem the endeavor a failure. He will not see the other possibilities now presented. He will not appreciate the new surroundings the leap has brought him to as a new opportunity to discover new aspects of his self, his circumstances, and the world he lives in.

The Fool however, will know that there is no set outcome to this leap. There is total surrender in his intention. He will see the benefit of the outcome of his leap of faith no matter what, be the landing gentle and soft, or be it a horrendous crash to the rocks below.

No matter what, he knows there is something to be gained. What though? What will he get out of this? He may not have an answer. He may simply know this leap needs to happen. What does he find upon landing? Half the fun of the leap is discovering just that.

The Fool will follow his gut instincts. Period. If his gut says jump, he jumps. If his gut says stay put, he stays put. If his gut says go here, go there, go somewhere, that is what he does. A fool knows. He just knows. If there was nothing to be gained, his gut would not be speaking to him. So, if his gut is speaking, he listens. How can he go wrong this way? There is no wrong. There is no right. All there is, is… is. And that is perfection. No matter what.

There is value in all circumstances, even the ones you do not hope for. An Idiot will close his eyes to this and mourn for the loss of his perfect ideal should anything less be the final outcome of his ambitions. This is an unfortunate mindset, for it leads to stagnation. It roots one in a dark box where it is impossible to see the sun peeking over the rim.

A Fool however, will never find himself in such a box. His mindset and attitude simply don't allow for it. Being boxed in is the result of inflexible mind- a mind that does not bend to accommodate new paradigms and ideas. In his flexibility the Fool is always going in the right direction. The spirit of a fool is a free spirit. It is not imprisoned by rigid thoughts.

 A free spirit is an unburdened spirit- a spirit without weight or shackles, a spirit that is not bound to that which saddens or angers it. This is the spirit of the Fool- a light spirit, a spirit not made heavy by the ego's weighty cargo, a spirit made light by the setting free of that which does not serve its highest good. When all that does not serve the spirit is cast off, that which remains is the truth. Follow this truth. This truth is your path to your personal perfection and enlightenment.

It is the Fool's path- a noble and divine road that will take you to where you need to go, wherever that may be. It may be an uncertain road, but it is not a scary one. Any fear simply indicates new horizons are being reached. Maybe you can't see your feet when you are on this road. A true Fool, a true wanderer of light, would not be concerned. Just trust. If your intuition tells you, and you wouldn't be on this road if you intuition didn't tell you, then that means you are headed in the direction you need to go. Not knowing what direction you should go, how can any direction be wrong? Not knowing what should be done, how can any actions be inappropriate? Not knowing what can't be done, what can't you do?

Not knowing any better, the Fool will do things he is not capable of doing. Nobody tells the Fool's heart what it can't do, so the fool does it. Or maybe somebody did tell the Fool's heart the things it couldn't do, but the Fool, hearing, chose not to listen and did these things anyway. The Fool is capable of a great many things undoable and unknowable to others because he is unaware of, or unaccepting of the things he cannot do. He does this without ego or any awareness that what he is doing is special in any way and seen as incredible to those watching. To the Fool, "impossible" is simply business as usual.

To put the ego in your rear-view mirror as you travel along the Fool's path to enlightenment is to become an example to others that it can be done, and proof that the spirit knows better than the mind what the body needs. It is proof that change need not be feared. Change is necessary. In change, enlightenment can be found. Just understanding that if something doesn't feel right in your life, it should be re-examined, readjusted, and redone can make a world of difference. It can be hard to realize this though. So, to see that somebody else has done it can be inspiring. It is your job, as the Fool, to provide that inspiration. Make the changes that need to be made. Prove it can be done. Show the way. Blaze the path.

When stuck on a problem, ask, "What would The Fool do?" The answer is the truest and most pure wisdom, for the Fool will see right through into what is real and honest in the situation. The Fool will not be taken in by the masks of ego and expectations. The Fool will see the heart of the situation. "What would The Fool do?"

So be the example! Be willing to make mistakes as you figure it all out. Understand that you need to be a complete Fool to ever achieve enlightenment. Be willing to set out on a path not knowing where the path leads or even why you are on it. Be willing to trust your faith and your inner voice. Know that even in hardship there are lessons that are being learned. Know all in the knowing of nothing. Value silence as well as noise. Be sure of your steps even when you can't see your own feet. Know that nothing is for nothing in the universe, Know that everybody and everything has its purpose even when no logical sense can be made of it. Fear not the journey. Fear not the idea of the journey. Be an alchemist, transforming fear into opportunity. Be willing, if necessary, to go it alone. Never be blind to the humor of it all.

19

Be a Fool for others! Show them the way! As a Fool, it is up to you to remind people of the amazing and infinite possibilities that exist for them. When they are in doubt or feeling uncertain, help them to see things clearly. What would a Fool do? Remember, the Fool approaches the situation without a preconceived notion as to what it is or what the outcome should be. The Fool will, without a doubt, offer a fresh perspective every time.

Where thoughts are rigid, so are attitudes and your perceptions. As a Fool, keep a soft and flexible mind. This will help to see through the cracks of rigid thinking to see the situation in a new light. Follow no prescribed spiritual path. Create a path blazed by you.

Watch. Observe. See what fits for you and incorporate these things. Answer to no one but your higher self. Share what you know but do not preach. If your knowings fit another's doctrine, that is wonderful. If it does not, that is fine as well. Seek no controversy, only acceptance and understanding. This is a Fool's spirituality. As a Fool, be a friend to all and share your genius. This will not only help you, but will also inspire others to embrace their own inner Fool and allow their inner light to shine.

That is something this planet needs- all the Fools it can get. Think about it- so many Fools, all escaping the traps of the ego and social conditioning, all marching down the path to their personal enlightenment with their own songs playing in their head, not the song society says they ought to be listening to, but the song that brings them the most joy.

Perhaps this is what it takes for the human race to evolve- all the Fools it can get, all elevating the vibration of the planet through the achievement of their own bliss. This is the evolution of Fools. Be a part of it and be proud. It can be a glorious thing.

Become enlightened by becoming a Fool.

Ask Yourself:

- How willing am I to follow my gut and operate on pure faith?
- Must I control the outcome of every event?
- Am I flexible in my thoughts and attitudes?
- Am I open to learning from every circumstance?
- Am I able to laugh at myself?

The Magician

1

Key Words

Manifestation
Clarity
Gratitude
Miracles
Law of Attraction

Here we see manifestation in progress. Where there was nothing, now there is something. You asked for it, so the universe is providing. Did you mean to ask for it? Do you really want this? The universe provides for you in the material world what is in your heart, so be mindful of what you keep there.

Your inner Magician is astutely aware of the holistic nature of your environment, both the internal environment, as well as the outer environment in which your earthly vessel lives. With this awareness comes a knowing of what is necessary and what is missing, as well as the intrinsic knowledge of how to manifest what is not there that should be.

What is magic? Magic is anything above and beyond the earthly and mundane. This is not mere illusion. Illusions are just that- illusions. They represent trickery and manipulation of perception, sometimes for entertainment, sometimes not. This is not to be confused with magic. Magic is a force of the divine as perceived by us in earthly form.

A magician is one who can tap into those divine forces and bring them to the earthly plane of existence. It is all in the asking. It is all in knowing how to ask. It is all about being heard. Speak to the divine from the heart. This is how they hear. They know by scanning our hearts, which hold our true intentions. Put your sincere desires in your heart and they will be heard. Ask from your heart and you shall receive. A true magician knows this.

A true magician is wise. Wisdom and manifestation are joined. Manifestation stems from the desire for what is lacking. How though, can you know what is lacking without knowledge of the whole? You see what is missing. You know what is not there. This is the root of desire- to manifest that which is lacking. This is wisdom.

Wisdom is to have the truth in your heart of what is entire and what is whole. Once examined, once a scan of the entirety is complete, one can see the gaps and the missing pieces. Now what is lacking is known. Now manifestation can happen. A desire to fill these gaps is the manifestation of manifestation. This is the gift of any true magician.

What does it mean to be a magician? A magician is somebody who is adept at creating something from nothing. A magician can ponder his needs and magically bring them into the earth plane. It may seem miraculous to the uninitiated eye, but in reality it is simple to do. So simple in fact, anybody can learn the trick to it. What is it really? It is simply the Law of Attraction.

The Law of Attraction tells us, "That which is like unto itself is drawn." What does that mean exactly? It means that like attracts like. What you emanate is what you will draw into your life. Therefore, consider what you want in your life. Now, feel the sensation of having it. Feel this sensation so strongly that it is as if you already have it. You are tricking yourself into believing that is already there. Now, like will attract like. The reality of having this will align with the sensation of having it, and then it will come to you.

This really does work. Practice at it. Once you start seeing the results, once your desires become increasingly manifested, it will become second nature. Soon, you won't even have to consciously think about the act of manifestation. It will be as simple as breathing, blinking, and circulating your blood.

As a magician, believe in yourself. What is your attitude? Do you believe you can accomplish anything? Are you telling yourself that you can do anything you set your mind to? Is it in your heart to accomplish all you wish to?

Being a powerful manifestor, it would be supremely wise for you to get really, exactly clear on what it is you want. Do not rely on vague concepts when establishing your intentions. Vague and unclear just won't cut it. The Universe wants to provide for you. It is able to and it genuinely yearns to, but you need to help it out by being exact and to the point about what it is you want.

Maybe you say you want to manifest "clarity." Okay, that's nice, but what does that mean? Clarity on what exactly? Let the Universe know. Clarity on life direction? Clarity on career options? Clarity on a relationship issue? What? What do you want? Focus on that. What you understand about this is what the Universe will provide.

Maybe you want to manifest a new car. Okay, that's nice. But what kind of car? If you don't know the exact make and model, that's okay. But what style do you want? Stick shift? Automatic? Four seater? Six seater? Flashy? Practical? Red? Black? Green? Focus on how this car will make you feel. Feel this. Feel it as though it is real. Feel it as if it is parked outside right now and you are about to get in it and go for a drive. Hold onto this feeling. The Universe senses what you are feeling and provides the actuality to match the feeling, a car just as anything. Therefore, be mindful not to cling to negative feelings and attitudes. Do you want more of that which you do not want at all? No? Well then don't cling to negativity. If something bothers you, let it go. Otherwise, you are attracting more of the same by keeping your attention on it.

Be mindful, too, of the power of gratitude in the manifestation process. This signals to the universe that you are aware of what it is that you are receiving. "Thank you." These are two very powerful words. Through "Thank you" the universe knows that you are aware of what you have received and will gladly provide more.

"You're welcome." These words are equally as powerful a force and an intention of gratitude as "Thank you." By saying 'You're welcome" you are enabling the gratitude process of another. Don't underestimate this. When one is putting out the energy of gratitude to draw in abundance to their life, it is amplified when they know the gratitude has been well received. A heart-felt "You're welcome" accomplishes this.

To gain confidence as a magician, keep an intention journal. Begin each day by writing your intentions for that day. Consider the day ahead, what would you most like from this day? It will also benefit you to consider the week, month and year ahead as well. Doing this daily, though, has the benefit of being very precise. It is easier to stay focused and allow for the subtleties of shifts and changes, and for the assessment of manifestations. How is it coming along? Do you see your daily intentions becoming manifest? As a magician, you are aware of your true power. Use this power. It serves you well on the path to your personal enlightenment.

Ask Yourself:

- Can I clearly visualize the culmination of my desires?
- Do I have confidence in myself?
- Can I clearly articulate my wants and needs?
- How much gratitude do I show?
- Am I generally a positive person?

High Priestess

2

Key Words

Intuition
Truth
Absolutes
Psychic ability
Pure knowledge

The absolute truth is not constructed by the mind or the ego. Are you ready to face it? The High Priestess will share it with you if you ask, but to face it as it is, or deny it because it is too difficult for you, is your decision alone to make.

Your inner High Priestess not only knows the truth, but knows the meaning and value of truth. A true High Priestess will not attempt to alter or temper the truth to fit her needs or desires. No, she will examine and accept the truth as it is and adjust her mindset and her paradigm to it, not the other way round. What is "truth?" Truth is an intrinsic state of being. It cannot be altered, and at its perfect best it is not open to debate. But how easy is it to get past the projections of and the assertions of the ego to get down to the core nugget of this truth within ourselves?

We can examine a situation, a feeling, or an attitude all we want and project our thoughts and our judgments into it until it is saturated with these things and examine the "truth" of it with all these additives obscuring what is at the heart of it until we are satisfied with what we believe to have found. But is this real?

The true truth has no such additives. It is perfect, but can at times seem cold and ruthless. That is because it is not tempered. We must examine this real truth without tempering it to suit our needs, our hopes and our desires. This is seldom an easy thing to do for it requires a surrender of ego. Those that can examine the truth truthfully have the benefit of authenticity.

With an authentic paradigm; you can approach and present yourself to the world accordingly. Examine the truth and don't shy away from it. How do you find this authentic truth? How do you differentiate it from ego and self-centered desires? This is never an easy task. Is it even possible? It is much easier to do with a quiet mind. Meditate. Explore your inner landscape for the answers. You will know it is a pure answer when your mind is quiet, because a quiet mind is not likely to attach its own needs to it. So quiet your mind and search. When you find what you are looking for, trust.

Will it make absolute sense at first? Don't expect it to. Once the truth is found, the mind will do what it can to attach its own meaning to it. This is why we must trust that what we found within is pure and perfect. This is what we call "intuition." Intuition is knowing without ego. What our intuition tells us may not be what the mind wanted to hear. Don't let the mind talk you out of believing it though. The mind has an agenda all its own. Learning to trust your intuition and your gut instincts will propel you far ahead on the road to personal enlightenment.

What do we mean by "gut instinct?" Intuition is seldom perceived in the mind. Don't you generally sense it in your gut first? It is these gut feelings that your mind then tries to interpret. "Where is this feeling coming from?" You ask. As you learn to identify where these feelings come from, you use your mind until it becomes second nature to just simply know. You will likely go through a period of trial and error as it begins to make sense. The more you understand and can make sense of the various impulses, the more you will find that you have them and the more you will be given.

Remember, intuition has an intelligence all its own. How could it not? Intuition is guided through spirit. Does spirit operate through the mind? No, it does not. It is the burden of the mind to try not to guide intuition, but rather interpret it as it is received from spirit. Is intuition ever perfectly interpreted given that the mind is clouded by the ego and thus subjected to the projections there of? When an intuitive impulse is received, accept it without giving thought to it. Otherwise it is subject to misinterpretation.

By way of personal example, I can say this- I learned to trust my own intuition when I tested it during a Trance Dance ritual. During a Trance Dance, you dance blindfolded. As I danced, my intuition told me that if I keep dancing to the left, I would trip over somebody sitting on the floor. Sensing this, I could have veered away. Gone another direction. Stopped altogether. But I kept dancing to the left. I had to know. Was there somebody there? Was my intuition providing me accurate information? Yes. It was. I tripped over somebody sitting on the floor just like my gut instinct said I would. Had I veered away, had I gone another direction or stopped altogether, I wouldn't know with accuracy that my intuition was correct. But it was. Now I know.

This is "Negative Intuition Testing," proving your intuition by providing the negative outcome of your impulse. There are two possible outcomes to listening to your intuition. There is the positive outcome, what you receive if you listen to and follow your intuition. There is also the negative intuition outcome, what you receive if you do not listen, or maybe you do listen but do the opposite of what it is telling you, like, "Dance in another direction. You're about to trip."

Sometimes we have to validate our intuition by proving the negative outcome because that is the simplest way to see the result. Had I not danced towards that person that I sensed was there, how else would I have proven to myself that there really was somebody there? Without tripping over this person, my intuition would never have been tested. How would I know that my intuition was valid? In the sense of the ego, I would not have known. So, there is a lesson here, and one I think that was not painfully learned. I didn't get hurt tripping over this person sitting on the floor during a shamanic blindfolded dance ritual, and I didn't hear anything about that person being hurt either.

So do this in the beginning of your intuitive experiments. Achieve the negative outcome of what you know without seeing. Consider what you know as "Other Wise." "Other" meaning separate from yourself, your mind, your ego. "Wise" meaning simple knowings. Become an "Other Wise" individual by validating your intuition. Once you know that it is valid, simply trust. Trust that somebody is there that you will trip over while dancing blindfolded without actually having to trip over them to prove it to yourself that they are there. Trust. Get used to trusting. Now that you know what you are capable of, take it to a grander perspective. Use it while navigating though not just a blindfolded dance floor, but through life. If you know something is right, it is right. This is one of the main lessons of the High Priestess. Master it, and life gets that much easier.

Ask Yourself:

- Do I trust my gut feelings?
- Do I pay attention to my intuition?
- Is my ego in the way of the truth?
- Am I seeing the big picture?
- Am I being honest with myself?

The Empress

3

Key Words

Fertility
Nurturing
Caring
Creation
Growth

The seeds you plant are what will grow. Do you have a garden of weeds or of affirmations? How do your deeds, actions, and words effect your life? The life of others?

Your inner Empress is keenly aware of her ability to take of herself and create. She, like the magician, has the power to conjure something from nothing. The difference being, while the Magician conjures from the divine onto the earth, her manifestations come from elements that are already present. Often, her own nurturing qualities and elements of herself, that when conjoined with other elements, create something new. This that is new may be life itself, as fertility often comes to mind when considering the Empress, or perhaps it is new ideas, mindsets, and attitudes.

A true Empress is adept at nurturing. She will hold close to her that which is growing and provide for it the elements necessary for its strength and power until she is confident it can survive on its own. The truth of this can take many forms, both tangible and intangible.

Consider the idea of gestation. A life is being formed and strengthened. It must be nurtured, cared for, and monitored until it is ready for the world. If you let it out too early, it will likely lead to tragedy. Consider your ideas in this same manner. Don't give them away too soon. Think them through. Consider them from all angles. Make sure they are as strong as they can be before unleashing them to the world. Visualize what you see these ideas growing into. What do they look like at their greatest glory? What do they look like beyond their greatest glory? Once your ideas are strong, they are ready to grow. They are ready for the influences of the outside world. It is time to birth these ideas. Give them to the world. Let the influences of the world help them to take shape and become what they will become.

Tap into your own nurturing side. Nurture yourself. Nurture your dreams. Nurture your ambitions. Pause and think for one moment- what have you been neglecting within yourself? What dream, what goal, what passion have you not given enough attention to? These things never die within you. They may become covered over with other concerns, but they stay with you. Look within and find some such thing that you have not given attention to and resurrect it. Treat it as a seed.

If you were to plant a seed for a plant you would like to see grow, would you simply stick the seed in a pot of soil and forget about it? No, you would water it. You would put it in the sun. You may even provide fertilizer to coax it into sprouting. Treat your rediscovered dream or ambition much the same. Bring it to life. Give it what it needs to grow.

Tap into your inner Empress. Step outside and appreciate what nature has to offer and be inspired by the trees and plants you see. Let each one remind you of a dream you are nurturing. Maybe you have a backyard. What can you enjoy in your backyard? Get out in it and get your hands dirty. Pull some weeds. Dig in the dirt. Look for treasures. Whatever. It doesn't matter what you do, just connect with the earth.

Maybe go to a park. Breathe in deeply the air. Hug a tree. Smell a flower. Plant some herbs. Gaze at the clouds. Go for a hike. Walk barefoot. Feel the ground beneath your feet and appreciate the connection you have with the earth. The earth is a good place. Enjoy your time on it. Enjoy your time by growing, expanding, witnessing your dreams coming true.

Tap into your inner Empress and plant the seeds that will grow into your dreams. Nurture them and care for them. Do not forget them. Let your ambitions sprout and grow strong.

What you plant is what will grow. Plant a watermelon seed and you can expect a watermelon to grow, right? So if you don't want a watermelon, don't plant that seed. If what you want is a pumpkin, plant a pumpkin seed. Consider this as you pursue your ambitions and create the life you want to live. Do you want a positive life, or a life filled with negativity? What is your mindset? Stay positive if you want a positive life. It is that simple. This is the seed you are planting in your soul.

Consider too your words as seeds that are being planted in the hearts of others. What do these seeds grow into?

Your words plant themselves in the fertile soil that is the heart of another. These seeds grow, nurtured by the thoughts and attention the person who's heart it has been planted give it. Keep this in mind when you speak to and speak of other people. Are you planting weeds? Poisonous plants? Or are you planting nourishing and refreshing plants that will grow into full blossomed positive self-images and attitudes? Speaking words to somebody that will make them doubt their selves or shrink away is to plant the seeds of weeds in their hearts.

To bring forth the qualities of the Empress, be sure to plant seeds in the hearts of others that will benefit them in their life. Plant seeds that will grow into positive life affirming beliefs and thoughts about themselves. Do not plant weeds. This is so of the words you speak as well as your actions around people. Be mindful of appearing aloof or distant. This will plant bad seeds just as sure as negative words spoken will. Give others your attention, your focus. This will signify that yes, they are significant. These seeds will grow into positive affirmations.

It is also true that these seeds often grow as a dandelion will, scattering in the wind, spreading outward in many directions, spreading the energy of the words to the hearts of others.

Consider your own heart. What seeds have been planted there? What is growing in your garden? Is it the crops of abundance you were hoping for? If not, why isn't it? What did you plant? Remember, what is growing there is growing there because you allowed it. This is your garden, not somebody else's. If you are unhappy with what is growing in your garden, weed it to make room for new growth. Be careful to plant the seeds that you most want to see grow.

Close your eyes and imagine that you are in a garden. This is your garden. This garden is your soul. So many things are growing in this garden. So many things have grown. It is a very crowded garden. There are flowers. Many many flowers. They are beautiful. These flowers are the positive aspects of your life, the things that make you happy in the here and now. Notice though, that there are a great many dead flowers as well. These are old thought forms and ideas that served their purpose and served them well, but are no longer valid to you as you are now. Your garden would be much better off if you got rid of them. See yourself pulling these dead flowers out of your garden and tossing them into a compost pile.

Notice also that there are a great many weeds in your garden. These are negative thought forms and ideas planted by other people. They do not belong in your garden, for they feed off the nutrients and the light that are meant for the flowers. You definitely want to get those out of your garden. See yourself pulling these weeds from your garden and tossing them into the compost pile. As much as it is possible, get these weeds out by the roots, even if you have to struggle to do so. Remember, non-native plants have shallow roots and shouldn't be too hard to pull up. Once you have a large compost pile, mulch it and use it to help your flowers grow, mindful that through pain comes growth and inspiration.

Be sure to tend the garden of your soul frequently. Don't allow for negative weeds to choke out the flowers that are your highest potential and contentment. Meditate frequently on your inner Empress. Take note of what you are creating from yourself in this world. Is it positive? If so, good job. Keep it up. If it is negative, ask yourself, "Why am I doing this?" And here, be completely honest. What can you do to turn it around and be more positive?

We are co-creators of the world we all share. Remember this and do your part to keep weeds to a few in the grand garden of the universe by keeping them few in yourself, and not planting them in others.

Ask Yourself:

- Do I generally make people feel good about themselves?
- Based on my attitudes and actions today, where do I see my life going?
- Do I cultivate positive attitudes?
- Am I spending enough time in nature to satisfy my soul?
- Is my own happiness being nurtured?

The Emperor

4

Key Words

Authority
Grounded
Role Model
Unwavering
Fair

A strong leader will set his own ego aside and lead for the good of the group. They will be respected for their ability to harmonize and synergize a group. They will be firm yet flexible enough to allow for new developments and ideas.

Your inner Emperor is grounded. He is rooted solidly into the earth. He, as an un-swaying, unwavering person is the authority figure. Ideally, he will be open to the ideas and feelings of others, but will take into consideration what is best for all and not be wishy-washy. The Emperor is a leader and must be able to make quick decisions and stick to them.

The Emperor will release all feelings of inferiority. As an Emperor, embrace your own power and emerge as a warrior butterfly from the cocoon. This does not mean a need to dominate others. Have a simple understanding of your own power as you relate to yourself and how you relate to others. Understand the energetic wave you ride. What do you uniquely contribute to the collective whole? How does your individual and unique self contribute to the collective consciousness? This is your Emperor quality.

Do not rely on old beliefs, patterns, and ways of doing things. See these as crutches that are used by the weak. Crutches are there for those unable to carry on without such support. The Emperor finds strength within himself without the use of flimsy support systems.

As an Emperor, examine your own strengths. Are you willing and able to stay true to your own ideas? Are you willing and able to consider others without being dominated by them? Are you willing and able to step up and be the leader when the need calls? Is your authority fair and balanced? Are you taking into consideration what is best for all? Are you flexible and able to consider new developments into a plan? Things change all the time; can you change yourself and your ideas to keep current with the latest developments?

These are all qualities of a strong leader. Do you possess these? When considering what it means to be an Emperor, think of somebody who is an authority figure, a rule maker. At the same time though, think beyond that concept. Yes, the idea of an Emperor does conjure images of power. This is most certainly somebody who is in charge and in control of a situation. It brings to mind a person who is looked up to and respected, but there is more to it than that. Being in charge can mean more than mere authority. Dig deeper in your thoughts of this concept.

See it not just as a power-figure, but as somebody who genuinely cares.

This can be somebody who is in a position to use his power to genuinely and positively affect another person's life.

Think about the fatherly qualities of the Emperor. What brings out the quality of nurturing in you? What are you doing when you feel you are doing the best for another person? How do you genuinely enhance the growth and wellbeing of others? What are you doing when you feel you are making the greatest difference? This is just as important when considering the qualities of a rule maker, boss, or authority figure.

When considering your Emperor qualities, ask yourself in what way you are looked up to? What wisdom and experience can you share? How can the life you have lived, the life you are living, create security and wellbeing for those you care about? Take stock of those who look up to you, admire you, and depend on you. Take this into consideration and realize that you are a role model. Take this seriously. There are so many simple things you can do to enhance the life of those around you.

Ask Yourself:

- Do I make wise decisions?
- Am I flexible with my ideas?
- Am I a positive role model?
- Am I trusted?
- Do I go back on my word?

The Hierophant

5

Key Words

Teacher
Respected
Elder
Meditation
Channeler

Wisdom comes to us through a willingness to hear. Gather knowledge so that you may share it with others. No wisdom is arbitrary. What you know is of great benefit to the world. Gather wisdom abundantly and share it generously.

Listen… listen… listen… if you ever hope to hear. There is wisdom to be gained everywhere. Some of it is obvious, some of it is not. Whatever the case may be, everywhere there is something to be learned and lessons to be gained. Open yourself to the potential to learn from all things and all circumstances. This is what it means to be a Hierophant. The Hierophant is acutely aware of the wisdom that is everywhere. He listens to it. He incorporates it into the totality of who he is. He shares it with others.

The wisdom that is available to us all comes from somewhere. It is here for a reason. It is here to benefit your own life, as well as to be shared and known to others that their life too will be benefited. Where does this wisdom come from? Consider that it comes to us through divine sources.

There are a great number of divine helpers who present us with knowledge for our enlightenment. They know. They have a much broader perspective on what it means to be alive than we do on the earth and they want to share with us that which will help us in our trek to Personal Enlightenment. We must hear it though. We must see it. We must feel and experience it. Consider our divine team pushing us in the direction of it, hoping that we will notice it and pick it up.

We trust that what our limited perspective does not perceive is known by our team- our inner Hierophant. A good metaphor for this is when on the TV show *Survivor*, tribe members are blindfold and another calls to them, telling them which direction to turn as they steer them to objects to pick up. The blindfolded ones listen, follow the voice, and pick up the object that is on his path. They don't do it alone. No, they follow the voice of the one who can see it. They trust and find what is in their path to be found this way.

There is much our inner Hierophant and our team of divine helpers see that we do not. Ask that they steer you towards them, and they will. They will with absolute certainty. But you on Earth are required to do your part. Take the steps that are being called out to you. Listen. Hear. These are synchronicities. Do not shrug them off. They are real. Always.

Honor them and Honor your guides by following their callings. In so doing, you are steered towards wisdom and enlightenment, as are the others with whom you share your found-wisdom with.

Listen and you will hear. Do not dictate the medium of the message. Allow for it in any form. Perhaps it will come as a simple knowing. Perhaps you will overhear a conversation where somebody says exactly the message you need to hear. Maybe you will see a cloud formation in the sky that offers you a point of clarity for the feeling it inspires in you. You may hear a song on the radio that answers the question you have. Do you appreciate different modes of divination such as tarot, runes, or tea leaves? These too offer a voice to your wisdom. Watch for answers. Notice them. They are not for nothing.

Remember too, your inner Hierophant knows your Life Plan. In other words, he knows what it is you came to the earth to accomplish. He knows the milestones you have reached, and those that remain ahead of you. When it is time to go in another direction, he will nudge you accordingly. You will receive a call to action. This does not override your free will by any means. It is only a reminder of what you had already planned.

If you ignore this call to action, it will only repeat louder and louder, each time getting more intense until you finally acknowledge it. The voices will scream louder and louder until you finally listen and embark on your journey. But to embark or not to embark, this is completely up to you.

When listening to your inner Hierophant consider what impulses and intuitions you have been feeling. Does it feel like you are being nudged in a new direction? Consider it. It may be time to embark on a new chapter of your life.

Ask Yourself:

- Am I open to new ideas?
- Do I think I know it all already?
- Can I view my life as a series of milestones that I have reached and that will be reached?
- Do I look for life's answers?
- Do I pay attention to the messages that come my way?

Lovers

6

Key Words

Partnership
Appreciation
Love
Mutual Respect
Give and Take

Strong partnerships are forged by mutual giving and taking. There is an honest and true appreciation that one has for the other that is reciprocated.

A Lover in the truest sense of the word is keenly aware of the connectivity and oneness of all beings. Lovers are dualistic and sensitive to the needs of others and understand how they fit into each other's life. A true Lover is attuned to the messages of the heart and will follow its guidance over anything the brain may say.

"Love" is but a perception. It is a perception of perfection, which of course is entirely subjective. It is a subjective perception of how we perceive the divine. Be mindful of what this means to you. It is contingent upon your Life Plan, that is to say, what you incarnated on the earth to achieve. Love is felt when we feel supported in this endeavor. When we encounter another being on the planet that supports our intentions we feel love.

We feel a connection. We each have a spark of the divine in us. This spark is the fire of our passion, our mission, our true essence. We seek out others, whether consciously or not, whose spark is of the same frequency as our own. When we find them, we feel that their spark touches our spark. This gives a sense of oneness. We discover that through them, our spark intensifies. It adds fuel that creates a stronger burning of our inner fire. We desire this more. We want to be in the energetic and spiritual field of this person.

We sense that our own energy is adding to the fuel of their own spark, their own fire. It is not a drain to us. It feels right and it feels real. In this way, love is a synergy of giving and accepting energy. Energy in this way begets more energy. Love is to fuel another's spark. Sometimes this fuel comes in the simple manner of showing support. Let this other know that they are valid and vital.

Relationships and love are about giving, not about taking. They are not about what you can get out of a person, but how you can enrich their life. A good relationship is one in which both partners are equally willing to give, and are open to receive what the other is giving. Remember that giving is what makes the relationship strong, that is to say the other is strengthened by the giving process, and therefore it is imperative to their happiness and growth that you show gratitude and happily accept what they are offering.

A strong relationship consists of partners equally willing to give, with the only expectation is that the other will be enriched by it, and not what you yourself should receive in return. Let the other give what they have to offer. Accept it. Show gratitude for it. Be happy. This is a good relationship. If you have it, be glad. Be sure the relationship is truly based on this mutual giving and receiving, and not about taking or being taken from.

It is common to feel separate from others based on our individual missions and the individual path this mission has put us on. To encounter another who is obviously on our path with us and who understands what it means to be on this path is to be fueled with powerful energy. This energy is love. Whatever we can do by way of validation and support of another in achieving their Life Plan is love. The more selfless this is given, the stronger the energy of it is.

Therefore, make a kind act about the receiver. Do not make it about you by expecting something in return. By expecting something in return for a kind act you offer, you only dull down or deaden the effects of it. Express true love by expecting nothing in return. Expecting something in return will degrade the gratitude process of the one who offers the gratitude. Accept their gratitude without qualifying it with demands.

Accept but do not expect. By doing this, you enhance the sense that the other will experience of love. Now they are energized. This energy will carry them forward. This energy will enable ripples to go forth into the universe. These ripples will go forth into the universe and touch and effect more and more and more. In this way, it will be returned to you. Will you identify it as coming from the person you affected? You should not try to identify it as such. Do not have an expectation. Just accept what you receive and be grateful for its acceptance.

This is a product of the synergy that you yourself helped bring about. This is why we must show kindness to others. Appreciate those you love, but show love to all. We are all a piece, a part of a much greater whole. There are those who share with us a certain aspect of this whole. These are the ones we are naturally and magnetically drawn to. These are the ones who we will "fall in love with." These are the ones we will most want to enhance and support. But this does not mean dismiss and ignore all others. Show respect and appreciation for all.

Many on the earth misunderstand love. They mislead their designation of it with mind felt, ego-centered obsessions out of fear. They will mentally choose a person. They will declare this person as the one they are "in love with" but this person is not on their path. Their paths do not support one another, but their minds will not accept this. They feel that because their mind has declared it, it must be perfect and true, for their mind is where they dwell.

Their ego is what propels them, not their hearts, not their spark or their fire. This is detrimental. This creates a ripple effect of disharmony. Now, they are depriving their self the opportunity to express love for one that is on their path and supports their Life Plan. This hinders the other in doing the same. And what of the others out there who are truly on the path of them or the other they are obsessed with? They too are being slowed down and/or denied of what can and should be ultimately beneficial to them.

In an ideal and perfect sense, this will right itself, as the negative situation it creates tumbles and collapses. But the mind and the ego can be a powerful effector in this. In the light of fear, it will not let go or release. This will slow down the process of growth and evolution for those involved. When love is right, you know it. When it is not right, you know it. When you know it, accept it. Let it go if it is not real. Release it. Support your own growth and the growth of others by not clinging to what is false. When considering your Lovers quality, ask yourself "Does this person or this situation truly enhance my path in life? Do I support their's?" Be honest with your answer, and accept it if even it is not exactly what you wanted to discover.

Ask Yourself:

- Do my actions and attitude promote harmony?
- How connected am I to others?
- Am I a team player?
- Do I expect too much?
- Am I more selfless than selfish?

The Chariot

7

Key Words

Enthusiasm
Fired Up
Do it your way
Excitement
Determination

Here we see the Charioteer excited. He is fired up! He is determined! He knows exactly where he is going, and nothing is in his way of getting there. This is by the force of his own will. He is reaching his goals on his own terms in his own way.

Think about "Gonna Fly Now" the theme to Rocky. This is a great song for your inner Chariot. What beliefs about yourself are holding you back from becoming your greatest self? Surge past them. This is the power of the Chariot. Harness it and achieve your greatest good.

By the force of your own will, accomplish! Maintain an unrelenting determination to accomplish your goal. One who is truly attuned to their Chariot Power will tap into its energy without letting a single excuse take hold to influence the outcome. Get fired up! You are powerful!

Tap into your personal power, your energy source, your heart and your divine will and get your mind out of the way. Your mind is the conjurer of excuses. Your spirit is the holder of the truth about what you can do. Fire up your spirit and push past the mind to accomplish everything you set out to.

The Chariot is about movement and mobility. Ask yourself this question- "What fuels this movement for you? What is its engine? From what source does it have the energy to move?" This energy comes from you. This is your personal mobility. This is not about jumping on the bandwagon of others. This is not about waiting for somebody else to make the decisions about what should be done and how it should be done. No, this your personal power. This is about doing things your own way and achieving your goals by the force of your own ideas and your own power.

It is important to change your attitude from "Wanna be" to "Doer." A "Wanna be" lacks the conviction to get it done. A "Wanna be" sees himself standing outside the door of his dream. He is looking in wishing he had an invitation to walk through the door and enter into the world of dream fulfillment.

A "Doer" doesn't wait for that invitation. He just walks right on in and announces to all present, "Here I am!" It really is all about attitude. Don't ever forget that. Change your mind-set, change your life. It is true in every aspect of living. Don't believe that? Try it and see. This is what it means to master the Chariot.

To master the Chariot is to be a great achiever, an inventor. Think about this. When others say it can't be done, you will say, "What you talking about?" Be willing to look stupid as you figure it all out. Combine an unwavering determination to achieve your ambitions with the fired up determination of the Chariot, and you have a combination that can accomplish and prove anything. Think about this in terms of Thomas Edison, Benjamin Franklin, and Alexander Graham Bell to give a few examples of those who decided to laugh at the idea of "impossible" and were masters of the Chariot.

Let the Chariot remind you of your unlimited possibilities. If you are considering an idea, or pondering a goal, ignore any notion of "Can't be done." You know better than that. Prove the possibility of it simply by doing it. Don't be a "Wanna Be." Be a "Doer."

Our Inner Chariot invites us to examine our goals and our motivations. What we want, we can achieve! We can do it our own way without relying on others to do it for us.

Could it also suggest that we are not trying hard enough? Could it be telling us that we need to put more effort into achieving what we want? Is it telling us to quit making excuses and get busy? Yes. It can tell us these things for sure and for certain. But that's not all it is telling us. It is also telling us to quit procrastinating. It is telling us to quit sitting around and get busy. Don't wait for tomorrow. "Tomorrow" is a false prophet. Do not filter your dreams through "tomorrow." Find your dreams today. Experience them today. The filter of "Tomorrow" will only wilt them.

What we desire, we can have. Books have been written, and movies have been made about this. This is "The Law of Attraction," and it is very real. How does the Chariot relate to this? That's easy. Once we know what we want, we can put our all into obtaining it. But what happens when we just can't find that "oomph" to put into it? That's when we need to activate the Chariot and overcome this procrastination.

Procrastination is one thing that separates unsuccessful people from those who achieve success.

What is meant by this word "success?" One way to look at the notion of success is to view it this way- you have a vision of what you would like to achieve, and you set landmarks to gauge the progress you have made towards it. In this way, you are able to see tangible evidence that you are gaining this achievement. Procrastination will always keep this achievement just out of reach.

Procrastination is the mud that will keep the Chariot stuck on the road to success. Procrastination will keep you from seeing the road beyond the next hill. Procrastination will prompt you to say "I can't accomplish the next three steps because I haven't finished this one yet." Well then finish this one! One, two, three, you're done! Those that can break the bonds of procrastination are the ones that succeed in their goals, for by accomplishing that first step, they clear the way for the second and third. This is how goals are achieved. This is how success becomes manifest.

With the Chariot, we finally make up our mind what we want and we go for it. No more procrastination. Pretend tomorrow doesn't exist. Do it now. Right now! Do it, not only for the sake of having it done, but also to silence the doubters in their insistence that it can't be done. Maybe now they won't be so afraid to try for themselves.

Ask Yourself:

- Do I act on my inspirations?
- Do I procrastinate?
- Do I feel successful?
- Am I making progress?
- Do I want to achieve?

Strength

8

Key Words

Inner Strength
Determination
Personal Power
Facing Fears
Stand your-
Ground

Apply your personal power to any given situation. True strength is found within, beyond the realm of emotions.

If you find that the circumstances are difficult, remind yourself of this one thing- nothing lasts forever. Whatever hardship or pain there is, just know, it can't last forever. Has the sun ever gone behind the clouds and stayed there? Eventually, the sun comes back out and shines again. Remind yourself of this when faced with unpleasantness. It passes. It gets better. Find the strength to endure. Those that do, prosper. Those that don't are eternal victims. Choose Prosperity. Choose strength. Choose to be strong.

What is your personal strength? Those on the path to Personal Enlightenment have discovered this. They know their strengths. They know how to compensate for their weaknesses with what makes them strong. To know your strength is to be powerful. To be powerful is not be overwhelmed by anything life may throw at you. To be strong is the ability and willingness to give your strength to others when they are in need of it.

The strength card of tarot is classically depicted with an average lady holding open the jaws of a powerful beast. Consider this. These beasts are powerful creatures. They are capable of taking lives. Their roar is capable of being heard over great distances. They are often portrayed as proud and noble beings, not subjected to the control and manipulation of others. In the depiction of the strength card, however, they are brought under control by a seemingly weak influence- an average size lady.

Think about this imagery. What does it tell you about the nature of your true strength? It tells you that when needed, you are able to muster great amounts of it. You can bring under control the powerful inner workings of your earthly selves.

We have egos. We have thoughts. These two elements, when left un-checked, can demand much attention and seek to influence our lives. Of-ten, these elements are detrimental. True earthly power is to master these. This requires strength.

"Strength" can mean different things in different circumstances. It can mean the strength to deal with a disappointment. It can mean strength to deal with a loss or heart break. It can mean the strength to handle an unpleasant situation without losing your cool. It can mean the strength to keep your mouth shut when your words will only add fuel to a fire, or per-haps the strength to speak up when you must voice your opinion.

Strength means to remain rooted in a firm foundation no matter what the situation. Anybody can learn to maintain a Zen presence and a center of stillness when the conditions are conductive to that, but can you maintain these things when your environment is a little more inhospitable? To do so is true strength. Do not become bowled over and flattened by circumstances. Tap into your personal power. We all have it. Can you find it? Have you learned to use it? Stand firm and stand strong, but be flexible. Consider the viewpoints of others, but make sure they consider yours as well.

Strength can represent the fight of ego and spirit. As the ego roars so loudly, the spirit has to be even louder to be heard. The lady in this card has the beast by the mouth. She is holding it open, as if she has fought the fight to silence the ego. Consider the beast to represent this- ego. The woman represents spirit. The ego roars but the strength of silence, spirit, and fortitude can win the fight and be heard over it. Once you become the master of this, when your spirit can be heard over ego, then as in the words of Rudyard Kipling, "Yours is the Earth and everything that's in it…"

When considering your own strength, consider where your ego is in the decision making process. How is it affecting your daily affairs? Are your thoughts working for you or against you? What must you do to remain grounded and firm? Who is speaking loudest, ego or spirit? Are you standing your ground? Are you being fair and reasonable? Are you there for others? Is your personal interest represented? Are you seeing the situation holistically to consider all viewpoints? Just how strong are you?

Ask Yourself:

- Do I face my fears?
- Do I keep my ego in check?
- What is my ability to keep a Zen-like presence?
- How aware am I of my personal power?
- How well do I handle difficult situations?

The Hermit
9

Key Words

Introspection
Alone Time
Silence
Tranquility
Solitude

There is much wisdom to be found within, away from the crowd. Paddle your own canoe and follow your own inner light. Get away from expectations and truly listen to your inner voices.

Your inner Hermit is solitary figure, but he is not lonely. He values meditation, introspection, and looking within. The truly wise and truly enlightened people know that to explore their own inner landscape is to find a level of peace, contentment, wisdom, and strength that those who do not venture there are simply missing. A Hermit may, to the initiated eye, seem like a lonely figure, but the reality is, he is far from it. To be a true Hermit and benefit from a true Hermit's nature, one must be completely comfortable with solitude.

Isn't it true that we all need some time to our self once in a while? If you need time to yourself, then by all means take it. It is a basic human need, and the true Hermit never apologizes for it. Being around other people can be trying sometimes. Why put yourself through it if you don't have to? Withdraw. Retreat. Hide away. Get away from the crowd. Turn off your phone. Be left alone. Don't feel like you have to indulge another's need to vocalize. Their needs do not have to be met at the expense of your peace.

The Hermit may ask, "Where is the dignity in a constantly running mouth?" A Hermit is a quiet person who finds strength and wisdom from within. They do not constantly talk. They do not need validation. They do not need their ego fed. They are comfortable with alone time. They appreciate silence, even in a crowd. They know the value of quiet time and meditation. They may look in disdain at the overly talkative types.

There are all kinds of personality types on the earth, of course. Some personality types may be polar opposite of others. Some of these are obvious. Take for example quiet people- people who are perfectly comfortable with silence without a need to fill it with words for the sake of filling it with words. This is a true Hermit. What is the opposite of a true Hermit? That would be somebody with an incessant need to talk.

There are different categories of talk. There is the general conversation where all parties involved are equally engaged. In a perfect setting, no one person will dominate the conversation. Everybody will say what is on their mind to say, and nobody will feel drained by it. It will be a mutual sharing of energy that all involved will appreciate.

Then there is brainless chatter. A true Hermit will find this draining. Brainless chatter is the need to vocalize every minor thought that pops into your head. The brainless chatterer may or may not even be directing the words at anybody. They are just talking. "Oh, it's cold in here. I should put on my sweater." "Oh, that kitten is cute." "I should put sugar in my coffee… no, I don't think so. Well, yeah. I think I will." Somebody in the room with this going on may wonder if they are supposed to respond to all of it, or if it is okay to ignore it. The truth is it should be ignored. But when the barrage of brainless chatter is constant others in the room have to weed out the brainless from the important. Sometimes, something important will get overlooked. This is the danger of brainlessly chattering. A true Hermit may be driven crazy by it and just give up and ignore everything that is being said.

Another form of talk is the interrogation. An interrogator will mistake a constant barrage of questions with true conversation. If you are with somebody who does nothing but throw one question at you after another, and all you are doing is answering them, do you really feel like you are having a conversation or do you just feel tired? When this is going on, do you wonder if this person asking you all these questions is even going to remember any of it five minutes later anyway? A true Hermit might wonder that, as a true Hermit would probably prefer to be left alone rather than endure this.

This isn't a category of talk, but have you noticed sometimes that when a group of people are being quiet, inevitably one of the people in the group will intrude on the silence by mentioning that it is so quiet? "Wow! Nobody's talking! We sure are quiet!" Or in an attempt to be ironic: "Boy we sure are a talkative group, aren't we? Ha ha ha." A true Hermit will likely be offended by that, for in all honesty, it can be insulting to somebody who values silence.

There are numerous categories of talk, but one last one to mention here is the stating of the obvious. In a group of people, there will always be one to do this. If there is an unexpected noise, a true Hermit will take in the fact that there was a loud noise. It is so obvious that it doesn't need saying. Except somebody will say it. "Wow! That was loud!" The true Hermit may or may not respond, but they may think with a sense of sarcasm, "No kidding. Really? Wow. Thanks for clarifying that." There are so many examples of how this happens. "It's cold." "That tree is tall." "That car is fast." It goes on and on. A true Hermit nature will prefer solitude over being around such talkative people.

A Hermit may be seen as the strong silent type- a "still waters run deep" kind of person. They are deep and wise. There is a bit of mystery here, an unspoken call for respect. This is the personality of a true Hermit. It is what you see when you see a quiet person.

A talkative person may project the opposite of this. With an overly talkative person, they may project insecurity. In some cases it may be an obvious attempt to hide a perceived inadequacy. They glom onto one aspect of who they are, one they are comfortable with and force this on you. They become comfortable in this role. They are comfortable in the reactions they know they can get with these behavior patterns. Even if these reactions are negative, even if they are driving others crazy, they are comfortable in the consistency of it.

So much human activity is fear based. Few will admit to it even when it is completely obvious to them. The fear of change is the fear of the unknown. How many people are willing to walk through darkness without a flashlight? How many people are truly willing to explore their own shadows? The only light that will illuminate a shadow is absolute truth.

To fully accept an absolute truth about one's self can be one of the most difficult endeavors to undertake. To accept a truth about one's self can often lead to the necessity of accepting a lie about one's self. The shifting of the paradigm from living a lie to living the truth will require fundamental changes. A true Hermit may have figured this out about their self a long time ago. But how many others can face this? How many are comfortable going within to see what is there, and then embrace it fully? For many it is easier to mask it with the false projection of constant chatter.

What does it mean to give up beliefs and lies about yourself? It means to conjure courage and a willingness to quiet your ego. It is the ego that holds onto the lie. The ego is comfortable with the attention it receives interacting and experiencing earthly life through the filter and the distance that the lie creates. So, to be a constant talker is to keep one's inner truth locked in a box away from the light. It is to stay comfortable in the paradigm of the lie.

Not everybody is comfortable with their self, and that is okay. We are all on the planet together, and we each have just as much right to be here as anybody else, quiet or talkative. At times, the best a true Hermit can hope to do is to influence others, to be the calm that influences the storm. The best they can hope for is that their quiet nature may become contagious. They may hope that through their example, others will accept quiet as an acceptable state of being, and to do your own thing without the need of validation from others is perfectly okay.

As a Hermit, do your own thing in your own way without any expectations being placed on you by others. This is important. So often, we live a life where the expectations that are projected onto us become the mandates that we live by. We tend to forget our own missions and priorities as we become what others need and expect us to be. Get back to yourself. Do your own thing. Find your own bliss. Shine your own inner-brilliance without unnecessary and unwanted influences from other humans on the planet infecting and affecting you. Sometime we must tune out others so we can tune in to ourselves. What you find within will be amazing. Don't let others distract you from it. It will be the best favor you can do for yourself.

Consider crowds. They can be annoying. Imagine all that energy swirled together like a bizarre soup mix that you can't control the ingredients of. It's not always bad, there are lots of good people with good energy, but there are inevitably those unpleasant people who are so unaware of how their attitudes, actions, mindsets, thought forms, and ideas are creating energetic pollution that comes at the rest of us from every angle and direction.

This is particularly uncomfortable for highly sensitive people who experience this on a much higher level than others. It is no wonder we sometimes feel drained at the end of the day, just from going shopping or walking down the street. Sometimes we must take a break from all that and enjoy the day in our own way. You don't have to explain yourself. Make an excuse if you must, but have the alone time your spirit craves.

Sometimes this is the best way to be artistic and brilliant. It's hard to hear our inner voices and follow our inner impulses when we have other people nagging at us, demanding our time and attention, or just talking too much. So if you need your own time, take your own time. Even if this means something as simple as eating lunch by yourself instead of with your colleagues, you are entitled to it.

Your inner Hermit may question you, checking to see if your spirit has all the time and space it needs. Are you letting the demands of others get to you? Or are you enjoying the time to yourself that you need? Be honest with yourself about this, because it does make a difference to your overall well-being. A true Hermit knows.

To honor your Hermit nature, make this a daily practice- listen to and show gratitude for your inner voices. Do what you can do to eliminate distractions and annoyances and tap into your inner self and appreciate what you find. Is there a creative power within that wants to be heard? Listen to it. Is there a force of wisdom within that has something to say? Tune in and really hear it. Is there an intuitive force that has a message for you? It would behoove you to have a conversation with it and discover all it has to tell you. It is easiest to do these things when undistracted by the needs and concerns of others. Do what you can to have quiet time to listen to your inner voices. Step away from the influence of others.

Be nobody's demographic. Be comfortable living outside of the media's influence. Think about it. When you are not told what to like, what to think, what to eat, what to drink, how you should look, what you should wear, what you should listen to, what you should watch, then who do you become? When you are not consumed with the thought forms of mass media and the marketing strategies of business men, who are you? Who is the authentic person beneath it all? Can you define your spirit? Can you identify your spark? Just how much of who you are is determined by the marketers?

It can be disappointing being in a society that is obsessed with conformity, when you yourself are focused on authenticity. Society says do this. Society says get married. Have children. Make sure you go to a bar and get drunk frequently. Watch football on TV. Watch basketball. Care about who wins the World Series. Feel a sense of emotional investment in who wins the Super Bowl or wins an Oscar. Have you had a Big Mac lately? The powers that be at McDonalds would really like you to, and will hound you until you do.

These are the thing you are "supposed" to do. Society wants you to buy its beer and get drunk. Numb your mind. Don't ask questions. Accept unconditionally everything that is thrown your way. Have a Coke and a smile. Don't try too hard to have a real conversation. It's easier and more satisfying to rely on small talk. Simply repeat buzzwords. "What are you doing this weekend?" Does it really matter? Do you really care? Empty puffs of air. Senseless excretion of energy.

Save your words until they add up to something substantial. Keep it sincere. Just say "Hello." Say it with sincerity from the heart that indicates you truly appreciate seeing the person you are saying it to. Aim for sincerity of words over quantity. This is important. Keep it in mind. Small talk is the clip art of conversation. Are you content to follow the programming set forth by those long forgotten? Small talk is nothing more than a program to be followed. It has limited value, if any at all. Break free of this innocuous time waster.

Strive for authenticity. Be a true Hermit. Meditate. Go within. Who are you really when you are not following the programs that society creates? What are you really craving? Is it a Big Mac? Or is it tilapia? If you're craving tilapia, pay no heed to the last McDonalds commercial you saw, and find yourself a fish restaurant. It really is that simple. Authenticity has become a lost art in the age of media influence. True Hermits are the renaissance bringing it back to the mainstream.

Turn off your TV. Turn off your radio. Ignore those popup ads on the internet. Don't be told what to do, what to think, or what you can't live without. You already know the real answers to these questions. The answers you find within are way more meaningful than what a marketer will provide for you. Consider your authenticity. Are you marching to the beat of your own drummer, or are you simply a lemming following somebody else's interests, allowing them to profit from your indecision? Be authentic. Be real. Be true to yourself. Embrace the Hermit quality you possess and be yourself even if it makes others uncomfortable.

Ask Yourself:

- Am I comfortable with solitude?
- Does silence bother me?
- Can I appreciate alone time?
- How easily do I look within?
- Do my words carry substance?

Fortune

10

Key Words

Luck
Prosperity
Circumstances
Appreciation
Reactions

What does "Fortune" mean to you? If you can't define it for yourself, how will you know when you achieve it? Give it some serious thought. What dos it mean to you to be fortunate?

One's fortune is in what one has appreciation for. One who is truly on the road to enlightenment will take stock of what they have that brings them happiness without mourning for what is missing. When you do this, you realize that life is good no matter what. This personalizes fortune. This takes away fortune from comparison, which is only just the ego's need for more. When you consider fortune to be what is perfect and good in your life, and not what you have that somebody else doesn't, or if you feel like you are lacking because somebody else has something you want but don't have, then you are truly appreciating what life is really about.

We create our own fortune and our own luck based on our reactions to the situations of our life. When we look at unfortunate instances in terms of "bad" or "negative" then obviously we will say we are having "bad luck." Is it really that bad though? If we turn that around and look for the lesson to be learned, then we see that there is something positive in all things. Lessons are everywhere in life. Remember this. There is always more to learn. Those that feel they know it all are severely stagnating their progress on the road to Personal Enlightenment. Don't fall into this trap. Keep your awareness on what there is to learn, and how these lessons are coming to you.

Sure, something may feel negative in the moment, but in the grand scheme of your life it is part of what makes you stronger. What seems like "bad luck" is actually quite fortunate for you. It is important to not let yourself feel defeated, no matter what. Look for the positive and appreciate it.

Of course, when genuinely positive and great things happen in our life, we call this "luck." It is beneficial to show gratitude for it. By showing gratitude, you invite more. But what exactly is "luck?"

Luck is the alignment of desire and circumstances. It is completely subjective. What is it you were hoping for? What is it that you need? This for you will be completely different than it will for somebody else. Maybe you are a fisherman. For you, catching a really big fish is lucky. But what would catching a really big fish mean to a businessman? To him, luck may mean closing a big deal. Perhaps you are craving a Milky Way bar and out of the blue, somebody gives you one. You would feel lucky then, wouldn't you? Let's say your car is broken down on the side of the road and you don't know what to do. A Good Samaritan stops to give you a hand. Lucky? Of course.

We consider ourselves lucky when we receive something we are hoping for, or perhaps something completely unexpected that brings us happiness, help, or comfort. Large or small, whatever comes your way, be thankful for it. Show gratitude. Gratitude is, after all, the door to abundance. The more we express it, the more opportunities to express it will come to us.

Pay attention when fortune happens, but don't wait for it and don't expect it. Just let it happen. By expecting something, you only create an opportunity for disappointment. This is what the ego will do. The ego wants. The ego expects. Let go of wants and expectations, and suddenly the ego has nothing to cling to. Simply be open to what comes your way. You will be surprised at just how "lucky" you are.

Notice these things in big ways. Notice them in small ways. The more you notice them, the more will come your way. So pay attention to your fortunes, be they monetary, material, or simply good vibes. They are all valuable and they are all worthwhile.

Perhaps you yourself may be an agent of change for somebody. Don't be shy to share your talents, your resources, your time, your energy. What better way to appreciate and enjoy what you have than by sharing it with others?

If others need your help, find time to help them. What talents do you have that you can offer? Are you a healer? Offer your services to those in need of it. Are you a good listener? Be there for somebody who needs advice. What can you do for each other? What trades can you make? A tarot card reading for a massage? A Reiki treatment for tax advice? A poem for a ride to work? Fortune comes in many forms. It can be as simple as having something to offer. Offer what you can. What will you receive in return?

"Luck" and "fortune" can have as many definitions as there are people on the planet. Be sure to know what it means to you so you can appreciate it, however it comes, in whatever form it manifests itself for you.

Ask Yourself:

- How do I define success?
- What do I feel is missing from life, and what can I do to bring these things into my life?
- Do I compare myself too much to others?
- Do I see the great things I already have in my life?
- Am I thankful for what I have?

Justice

11

Key Words

Fairness
Balance
Legality
Contracts
Laws

Justice is dispassionate, concerned only with the rules of the given society concerned. She is not swayed by emotion or prone to prejudices.

To be aware of your Justice quality is to have an astute understanding of what is fair, right and balanced. This is to put your own needs and projections aside and zero in on what is perfect and true in a situation. It is to remove yourself and your needs and see from a much grander perspective what is right.

The Justice card is typically portrayed with a dispassionate figure wearing a crown of authority. She holds a set of scales in one hand, and a sword perfectly upright in the other. Behind her hangs a curtain strung between two pillars, seemingly to block the view of what is behind her from any onlookers. What exactly is going on in this picture?

Justice here is depicted in a similar fashion. Here, we see a stone-like statuesque figure with the scales of justice. She looks stoically beyond the bovine being, reminding us that true Justice is perfect and pure, beyond any B.S. that may be presented.

Also here, we see a forest behind her in lieu of a curtain. The truth of a situation lies just on the other side of it. The lady of justice will point you on the path through the forest, but only if you ask her to. As she points you in the right direction, it is up to you if you follow it all the way to the end or not. It may not take you exactly where you want to go, but if you want to know the truth, you must go. If you are more comfortable with denial and a false representation of the truth, then simply stay where you are. You need not make the journey. You need not bother Lady Justice. If your mind is already made up, what's the point?

Be mindful though, just because you are not open to the truth, others may be, especially when it comes to legal proceedings. The truth of Justice may be forced on you whether you want it or like it or not.

Why is Lady Justice dispassionate? First of all, she is dispassionate because she doesn't care. Whatever the outcome is, it is meaningless to her. All she cares about is what is right and just, based on the rules set forth by the individual society or community that she is considering. She has no personal investment in the outcome whatsoever.

There are certain exact truths decided upon by society. The Lady of Justice is the caretaker of these truths. She will examine the intrinsic nature of these truths, and when there is a dispute, she will render her verdict with cold and calculated sureness. Similar to the High Priestess, she is not concerned with the egos of those involved. She is concerned only with getting to the exact center of the heart of the matter. In this way, her decision will be balanced and fair, as indicated by the scales in her hand.

In tarot, the workings of the mind are often represented by the suit of swords. Lady Justice is typically depicted as holding her sword in perfect balance. It does not sway and it does not falter. She holds it perfectly straight. This indicates a keen mind. She is going to keep her focus on the subject at hand. She is not going to be swayed by emotions or the projections of others. She is keen and she is sharp. She will remain true and undeterred by prejudices.

She is the ultimate authority. What she says goes. Her decisions are not subject to arguments. She wears a crown on her head. This is the crown of authority. What she says is based entirely what has been decided upon by the society over which she governs. Her decisions are not arbitrary or unreasonable. She is simply the steward of society's decisions and governing system.

What is hidden behind that curtain behind her? What is at the end of the path through the forest? This is the truth. This is what has been rendered by society as perfect for that society. She is not keeping it a secret. It is not knowledge only for her to know. You need only ask to be shown it. You must go through her to see it; for through her all ego projections will be dropped. You must leave them with her. Taking the ego to the world of perfect truth will only muddle your perception. You will not get an accurate view of what is right and true. As the gatekeeper of these truths, she will not allow you to approach with any such skewed perceptions.

When examining your Justice quality, consider if the situation is fair and balanced. Is there anything you are forgetting? Is your ego and expectations clouding your judgment of what is true? Are there any legal details you need to tend to? Be completely honest with yourself on all these things. Complete honesty is key.

Ask Yourself:

- Am I fair to others?
- Are my decisions based on what is best for all involved, or is my ego in the way?
- Can I accept the truth even if it is not what I want to hear?
- Can I see past the projections of others to what is honest and real?
- Do I respect authority?

Hanged Man
12

Key Words

Surrender
Acceptance
Other Angles
Go with the flow
Perspectives

See beyond what is obvious. Don't get stuck in a mind-set that tells you things can be only one certain way. See things from many different angles. Rise above situations and see them from a new vantage point.

Your life is based on the decisions you make. The question becomes, how do you make decisions? Do you rely on the same thought patterns and analytical avenues that you always do? Do you keep your sights limited on the situation at hand, or do you expand to see it from a greater vantage point? Are you able to see it from other angles? Can you see a variety of options in every situation and incorporate them into your decision making process? Tap into your inner Hanged Man. Your inner Hanged Man is gifted at seeing all things from many different angles.

Much of life is in the lessons we learn by being present and aware on the earth. Learning the lessons presented by the circumstances we are presented with lead us to enlightenment. In pursuit of perfecting our spirit, we are given many opportunities to live a circumstance that is designed to teach us, and to lead us down the path of awakening. The trick is to recognize these situations as a learning and growth opportunity.

When we do this, we become fully realized beings. Your inner Hanged Man will remind you of this. He will remind you to examine the situations of your life from a different perspective. Instead of looking at the pain of a difficult situation, look for the lesson it can teach you. This will accelerate your growth and help you reach the light that much quicker.

To learn from a lesson, from a life situation is to graduate from that lesson and move on from it. If you do not learn the lesson that the life situation was designed to teach you, you will revisit the situation in other forms. Always be aware of life lessons. Examine situations as to ascertain the lesson to be learned. Really examine it. Ask for divine help in seeing and hearing the lesson if you do not sense it right away. If you do not learn, it will rise again in another form to try and be learned again. Remember this. Synchronicities are ever being created to bring these opportunities to you.

Often, you will be reminded of the original lesson opportunity in a dream. Examine the dream. Reflect on the dream and examine the situation that the dream is taking you back to. Find the lesson. Perhaps you were too close to the subject when you first experienced it, or were not of the mind set to examine it for a lesson. The dream gives you a second chance. The dream reminds you that there is something unfinished left over from the original occurrence, and unless you examine it now, you are heading into the next opportunity learn it; a new opportunity is under way in manifestation. If you examine the dream and figure it out, then perhaps the new lesson opportunity will not be necessary and your energy can be put towards new growth.

Think about it. How many times do you want to keep reliving the same scenario in your life? This is a normal thing to do we notice that the same thing keeps coming up, and we keep saying, "This always happens to me." Of course this always happens to you, and it will continue to do so until you experience it fully, get from it what you are meant to get from it, and become that much stronger for it.

What are you waiting for? The next time you catch yourself saying, "This always happens to me" look at it from a different angle. Ascertain what it is that you are resisting from it and incorporate this into your awareness. Now you have mastered this aspect of your life. Now you are not a victim of it, but a guru from it. This is the Hanged Man's contribution to enlightenment.

Those who are truly in alliance with their inner Hanged Man know to surrender and go with the flow. Going with the flow equals serenity. It allows for healing. When you are no longer struggling in the wrong direction, diverting your energy towards unnecessary points, your energy is free to go towards healing. To do this, you must allow your heart and your mind to soften. Do not be rigid in your thoughts. Allow for flexibility of ideas.

Do not be rigid in your heart. Allow for an even flow of energy inward and outward. What you have in your heart is of great benefit to others. Allow it to flow outward. Allow also for the energy of others to flow into your heart. This is to live fully.

"Allow" is the key word here. As you soften your mind and your heart, you allow in the divinity and the light that is your birthright to receive. Allow your spirit to guide your thoughts, not the other way around. Soften so that spirit will have dominion over ego. If you are used to letting the ego and the logical mind run the actions of your life, it is time to surrender and allow for the other way to determine what is true for you.

Consider the symbolism of the Hanged Man card. The upside down man of the Hanged Man can be seen as a reversal of the common way of perceiving and reacting. The man is upside down. In the card, the heart is now above the head, symbolizing spirit over ego. Try this and you will be amazed at the difference it makes in your life.

The word "surrender" is frequently used when discussing the Hanged Man. It means to stop focusing your attention on the ego and the mind- to cease production of the product that the mind and the ego produce- worry, anger, fear, doubt, insecurity, sense of importance. It means to let your spirit have its say. It means to accept that much of what you think is important, isn't really. It means to admit that much of what you think matters, does not.

It can be a difficult thing to do- to surrender to the flow, but once you are able to do this in whatever place and environment you are in, the sooner you are able to establish equilibrium. For that is what "surrendering" accomplishes. In the act of surrender, you establish equilibrium with your environment. The sooner you do this, the quicker you can just be happy there. Being happy where you are allows you to open your heart to others. You learn much about yourself, and therefore about the universe and your place in it through allowing others into your heart to explore.

Form an alliance with your inner Hanged Man. He is inviting you to see the world from another angle. Remember, you are gifted to see things and present them in a way other than how others are accustomed to seeing them. This will excite some. To see the example you set and make known that the option of another way exists can be thrilling.

Just as often, however, your inverted view of the world will frighten people. Fear turns to hostility some of the time, for the idea that things can be different is frightening to many people because it upsets the natural order of their life. Those that fear change will fight it, of course, and you, being the face of change, often you will bear the brunt of that hostility. If you can accept that, you will be a powerful force. Fight it, and you will be weakened. Live as you live. Be the example. Have no fear. Let the Hanged Man empower you.

Ask Yourself:

- Am I able to surrender to the flow?
- Do I have the ability to see things from a variety of perspectives?
- How aware am I of what is happening around me?
- What am I resisting that I should be accepting?
- Is my heart or my thoughts in control of my life?

Death

13

Key Words

New Beginning
Changes
In with the new
Metamorphosis
Renewal

Like the end of one chapter of a book and the beginning of a new one, so is death. Death is a metamorphosis from one state of being to the next. Just as a caterpillar emerges from the cocoon transformed into a butterfly, so too do we transform from one form to another as we grow and remain open to change,

Things change. This is one of the most simplistic and basic statements of truth that can be said. Think about yourself. Are you right now as you were a year ago? Two years ago? Ten? How did you transform from what you were into what you are now? You really had to let go of old thoughts and ideas to achieve complete metamorphosis.

To become the best version of yourself, you must be able to let go of what does not serve you, and embrace those things that do. Your inner Death quality reminds you of this. Don't think of the Death card as literal death. Think of it instead as transformation. For what is death but a transformation from one sate of being to another?

Consider the metamorphosis of the caterpillar to a butterfly. When you look at a caterpillar, it is hard to imagine that such a creature will one day become a butterfly. But it happens. The caterpillar commits itself to making this change, and it happens. At some point in the transformation process, the caterpillar officially crosses the line and becomes a butterfly. It has stored up its energy. It has undergone the stress and the pain of changing itself at its core level. Then it emerges.

Think about this in your own life. What goals have you set for yourself? How close are you to achieving them? When you picture the greatest version of yourself, what do you see? What are you willing to endure to become what you most wish to be? At some point, you will reach the point of no return on this endeavor, and you will be this new thing. Are you willing to devote yourself to it? Do you have what it takes to do what it takes? It's easy to remain a caterpillar. It takes determination and an ability to endure to become a butterfly. Can you shed your inner caterpillar in order to become something more grand? More significant?

Don't fear death. It is simply a releasing of old ideas and old processes that have served their purpose. Let them go so that you may fly as you are meant to. Don't let them weigh you down, and don't let them become excuses.

When pondering the metamorphoses of your own life, consider this. Consider what you are holding onto that you can let go of to transform into what you are able to become. What blocks are you creating for yourself? What excuses are you making? What actions can you take to get past these things and be who you are meant to be? What can you do to become that being you are programmed to become if only you can get past your own limitations? Think about these things and put a plan into action.

Death is about renewal, rebirth. This can take on many forms. It can be new respect, a new path in life, a new job, a new home, anything that represents the end of an old chapter and the start of a new. Most often, this change is welcome, even if it is a little nervous to ponder. Ultimately, it will work out for your best good.

Ask Yourself:

- Do I embrace change?
- Am I the best version of myself?
- What changes do I want to make in my life?
- What things, thoughts, and attitudes can I let go of?
- How committed am I to making the changes I want to make?

Temperance

14

Key Words

Blending
Alchemy
Balances
Harmony
Centered

Just the right blend of elements creates harmony in life. Just as a bee pollinates flowers, creating just the right blend of elements for growth to occur, so too should we endeavor to blend our energy with the environment at hand for the best possible balance.

Mastering your inner quality of Temperance is to appreciate the balances of life. Picture a level- one you use to check the evenness of a surface. There is that little bubble that you want to get right into the middle of that little glass window. This tells you that the surface is level. For true enlightenment, we want our spirit to be just as even. How do you do this? By monitoring your emotions, your actions, your reactions, and your attitudes. Don't let any of these things stray too far from your center.

Establish a baseline of who you are in terms of how you feel emotionally and spiritually. This is your center. When you feel distressed or under pressure, or that you have been pulled to another place that is uncomfortable to you, you have this destination to return to. Make this baseline a place of joy and happiness.

Temperance is about finding and creating just the right balance of elements to bring about harmony and a sense of perfection. Imagine you are going to take a shower. You turn on the water and it is too cold. You adjust it to create more warm water. Now it is too hot. You adjust it again. You keep adjusting and readjusting until the water feels just right. This is alchemy. This is temperance. You have tempered the cold water with the hot, the hot water with the cold, and now you have just the right balance of both. The hot and the cold are now in harmony with one another. This is balance.

Be mindful of your own Temperance by applying this principal to the energy you deal with in your life every day. Find just the right balance to maintain harmony.

Perhaps you are upset with somebody. You want to let the person know you feel this way. But first, ask yourself, "Why do I want them to know I am upset?" Is it to feel a sense of revenge? Will it make you feel empowered to direct your anger at them? Or do you wish to let them know you are upset in order to create a meeting of the minds, and come to an understanding with one another about expectations and boundaries, so that future harmony may be established in situations similar to that which caused you to be upset in the first place? If this is the case, it is wise to temper your anger with a dose of understanding and compassion.

If you approach the situation by screaming and attacking the other person, you are not creating an environment conducive to equanimity. No, you are creating a breeding ground for hostility. If you wish for peace and understanding, temper your anger with compassion.

Compare the Temperance card to a cake recipe. When baking a cake, you want to get just the right amount of sugar in relation to the amount of flour. This applies to all the ingredients. You need to get the right mix of everything in the recipe in relation to each other. If you got it right, you will have a cake that you will enjoy eating. If you get the proportions wrong, the cake will not be very good at all.

Once the ingredients are mixed together, they become a unified whole. You can't go back and take the egg out, or take out just a little of the sugar. No, once they are mixed, the ingredients become a new entity unto itself. This is equally true of the energy you put into a situation, as it blends with the energy of others. Once you put it out there, it is out there. You cannot take it back. So, be mindful of what you are putting into the mix. How well does your energy blend with energy of those around you? How are you contributing to or taking away from the general mood of the situation? Are you promoting harmony, or are you degrading it with negativity?

Understanding Temperance is also to understand your individual uniqueness. Let it remind you of this as you mix the energy you possess with the unique energy of others. This mix becomes a blend, which becomes an entity all of its own. What are you adding to the blend? That becomes a pertinent question.

Ask Yourself:

- How does my energy blend with the energy of others?
- Do I remain balanced and centered even in difficult circumstances?
- Can I differentiate between my own feelings and what I am picking up from others?
- Do I treat others with compassion?
- How well do I control my emotions?

The Devil

15

Key Words

Shadows
Bravery
The Dark Side
Hidden Self
Unexplored

To be the most authentic version of yourself, you must face your Inner Devil and slay it. This Inner Devil will take on many forms including limiting thoughts, past traumas, addictions, and fears. Face them to reach the new horizons of your life.

To get to the light, you must first explore your shadows. Enlightenment simply is not possible otherwise. There are countless ways to define "Enlightenment." There are many ways to gauge where we are in relation to the enlightenment you seek. In one sense, enlightenment can mean to be made less heavy, to have shed the weight that is keeping you from ascending to your highest potential.

What causes this weight? Unnecessary fear, addictions, limiting thoughts and attitudes do. Once you get past these, they fall away, and you are no longer bound to them, no longer tethered to the shadows holding you down.

Another way to look at enlightenment is to see yourself becoming filled with light. This light is the truth of our highest potential. When you are not convinced of what you cannot do, when you are not living with the programs of what is wrong or improper for you, when you are not clinging to the dead weight of past hurts, addictions, and feelings of guilt placed on you by others, then you truly bask in the pure and perfect light of who you are and who you are meant to be. In other words, when you no longer hide in the shadows, enlightenment becomes you.

The question then becomes, where do these shadows come from? The answer is; where do any shadows come from? Shadows happen when light is blocked. In the case of your inner landscape, consider this light to be the truth of who you are and who you are meant to be.

And what is the block? What is casting this shadow? These shadow casters are all the negative feelings, attitudes, and the addictions you acquire. in life, lifetime after lifetime. These blocks are not organic to your true nature. Dissolve them to indulge in your true light. Remove any block that is preventing it from shining on you.

Be an observer of your shadows, but do not get lost in them. It is easy to dwell in self-pity and memories of old hurts. Be careful not to do this. Keep a perspective on your shadows. To explore and understand them, you must rise above them to see them objectively. Observe your shadows and follow them to the source of their light to find what it is that brings you joy. Joy is bliss. Bliss is enlightenment.

How do you escape these shadows and become free of them once and for all? You do this by following the shadow back to the source of their light. A shadow would not exist if it were not for light. Shadows happen when light shines upon a block. These blocks can be disappointments- disappointments that led to feelings of inferiority, sadness and unworthiness.

You had an expectation. This expectation was light. Something kept this light from reaching you. This is the block. These blocks integrated themselves into your soul. They created so much darkness that there was nothing there to see but that darkness. These shadows became such a fixed part of your reality that you forget that there ever was such a thing as light. Many problems can be a result of this darkness, this shadow.

These shadows need to be explored to find their source. Start with what you know- how you feel. Ask "How do I know this? Why do I feel this way? What instigated this in me?" Find the answer and follow it backwards to the last time you felt it. Let every answer inspire the next question. How do I know that... why do I feel this way... how do I know that... why do I feel this way... how do I know that... why do I feel this way? Keep asking and retracing the steps until you arrive back at the source of the light that created the shadow. What was the initial source of the disappointment? Relive that moment, this time though, with a positive outcome. Feel it as if it really happened in this positive way. This will create a ripple that will extend to you in the present moment in which you feel good about the incident.

Shadows can also be filled with pain. This pain though, is resolvable. Just as you can re-experience disappointment to resolve it, so to can you re-experience pain to heal it. Remember, you can never escape your shadows because they are attached to you. Ignore them and they will drag you down, slow you down, and weigh you down. You can deny them all you want, but this does not mean they go away. Facing them makes them go away. Face them, deal with them. Integrate them. Only when you accept them as a part of who you are do they go away and you become light.

It is crucial to heal old wounds and old traumas. If they are not healed, they will continue to resurface and cause disruptions in our life. To do this, return to them and experience them. Experience them fully. Find them in your shadows. This is where you tucked them away. You didn't want to experience them in the moment they were happening, so you pushed them away and tried to forget them. This is a normal thing to do. We all do it. But this does no good. They do not disappear just because they are hidden.

They just lay in wait until they are triggered and can come back to you.

To heal from the pain, you must return to these shadows and bring the pain back to you so you can deal with it. You must deal with it fully and completely. This is crucial to living a full life. If you are uncomfortable doing this alone, then by all means seek the help of a qualified professional to help you through it. The pain that resurfaces can be nothing short of intense. Help getting through it can be beneficial.

How do you identify where an old wound or trauma exists? When you feel a hurt brought on by a situation that is so familiar to you, when it seems like this particular situation keeps repeating itself in your life, take a look at it. Really take time to examine it. Ask yourself what was going on the last time you felt this way. And the time before that. And the time before that. And the time before that. And the time before that. See if you can trace it back to a time in your childhood or to a time when you were a baby and look around.

What brought this on? What do you need in this old moment that you are not receiving? What is your perception of lack right here and right now in this past moment of wounding? What are you not receiving that you most need? The lack of this is wounding you. Most likely it is a sense that you are not receiving the love or compassion that you need. Examine this. As you examine this, allow yourself to feel the pain that you were feeling in that moment in time.

In the past, you did not know how to deal with it, so you just let it hurt you. You pushed it away as a natural reaction to it. But pushing it away, pushing it down within you did nothing to relieve the pain. This only left it unresolved. Because it was unresolved it continues, and will continue to continue to resurface. This will repeat itself for all the days of your life until you resolve it, until you fully experience what it was that you were feeling so long ago.

So use your memory even if your memory is unclear, and of course it will be after all this time. If you can, employ the service of a qualified hypnotist to lead you back. Put yourself back into the position and the place that you were in your first memory of this incident. Your first memory may or may not be the first occurrence, but for the sake of healing, it is as good a starting place as any. Give yourself a chance to go through it all again, but this time instead of pushing the feeling away, hold on to it. Feel it fully. Experience the pain fully. It may be intense, but ride it out.

What do you need in that moment? What would have made all the difference to you in terms of relief from the pain? Love? Send yourself some love. Don't be shy about this, and don't hold back. This is healing. This goes a long way towards fortifying yourself and generating strength.

When you find yourself repeating the same old patterns in your life, mediate on the Devil card. When you find yourself experiencing old pain and saying, "Here we go again" don't let it upset you. Get excited over it. Get excited because now you have a chance to experience it with intention. Set your intention to fully explore and experience the pain. Once you have experienced it, you have mastered it. You are now in control, not it. Now that you are in control, it cannot cause the grief it once did. Use the Devil card as a focus for your meditations into your unhealed past. It will be of great benefit to you, guaranteed.

Ask Yourself:

- What's bothering me?
- Why am I triggered by certain things and certain people?
- What do I need for complete happiness?
- What unhealed pain can I identify in myself?
- What is blocking me from being light?

The Tower

16

Key Words

Sudden Change
Purification
Gateway
Difficult Truths
Foundations

Sometimes it takes a huge jolt to put us on the path we are meant to be on. This jolt can seem like the end of the world, that all that is precious to us crashing down and that there is no hope. But there is hope. These are wrongs that are being set right as part of the natural order of life. Once past, life gets truly good.

The heart can never build a tower. Only the mind can. To understand this is to understand your inner towers without fearing them. Towers represents a situation in your life that is simply not meant to be. Your mind creates scenarios that seem so real and so perfect. Your spirit knows better though. Your spirit knows that no matter how alluring these situations may seem, they honestly do not fit your highest and best good. Your brain, however, doesn't accept the fact that this situation does not serve you, so it continues to pursue it. In this way, you build towers higher and higher, with their stability becoming less and less firm.

Towers are bound to tumble. They are not reflective of what is right and perfect for you, so how can they last? That which is not meant to be in life will fall away. Sometimes they will be blasted away. If you insist on clinging to ideas that do not serve you, you create tower incidents for yourself. That is to say, you are setting yourself up to have an eye-opening dramatic situation in your life. You are building a tower, brick by brick, with your false ideas about what your life is all about and what is in your best interest. Towers can be built by the bricks of wrong relationships, poor career choices, bad places to live… so many things.

Your mind has a hard time accepting that these things are wrong for you, so it keeps a hold on them. These ideas accumulate, one after another, after another, after another. Each one is one more brick added to the Tower. As more and more bricks are added, The Tower gets higher and higher, less and less stable until some fateful day it is blasted away in a "Tower Incident" to put your life back on the track it is meant to be on.

What is meant by "Tower Incident?" This is that point in time when your life can sustain not one more falsehood, not one more misconceived notion of what is best for you. This is when what is wrong finally makes an attempt to right itself. This is when spirit finally screams louder than ego, and the bricks encasing your Light are finally blasted away so your truth can shine freely.

The Tower is tied to expectations. An expectation is a desired outcome. Is this desired outcome tied to your highest and best interest? Or is it tied to ego? If it is tied to ego, of course this will become a Tower Incident. How do you overcome this? One way is by embracing the Hanged Man.

The Hanged Man reminds you to see a situation in a different way, from a different angle. When your Tower falls and you are left with the rubble, doesn't it make sense to look at the situation from a different point of view to understand why exactly it fell? If not, what happens? You just build the same tower all over again and you will be upset when yet again, it falls.

Identify and analyze the Tower when you find yourself in one. The Tower does not need to come crashing down if you identify it in time. Notice that you are in a Tower and cease building it immediately. What bricks built this Tower? Analyze them. What falsehoods contributed to it being built? Examine them. What is it about your life that simply feels off or wrong?

Not one more brick should be added. The sooner you identify the Tower, the sooner and more quickly you can vacate it. If you know a situation is a Tower, and that it will come crashing down with you inside, why are you still in it? Get out!

Getting out will take a surrender of the ego. To hold on to your ego while inside the Tower means you are making excuses for the fact that you are in the Tower to begin with. These excuses become denial. Every ounce of denial equals twenty pounds of brick that you are using to build the Tower. Remember, these bricks are going to crash down and bury you beneath them. But to admit that it is a tower you are in without looking for blame and fault means you can gently and quietly exit before there is a disaster.

In other words, when you know something is not right about your life, just admit it and make the necessary changes. By doing this on your own accord, you prevent a dramatic situation from forcing it on you. Don't look for scapegoats, and don't assign validation to others as for why you must live in a way that is not right for you. This may not be easy, but it is important none the less. Find the strength and find the courage, then do it.

This is the reason why embracing the Hanged Man will mean much fewer tower incidents. By surrendering, you allow for the flow of what is natural and meant to be. By struggling against the natural flow of what is meant to be, you are building a Tower. It will happen every time.

Be mindful of the Hanged Man too when your Tower falls and you reassemble the pieces. Only reassemble the pieces that fit. The pieces that don't fit never belonged. Those that do fit are the truth of who you are.

Put the pieces back together, but of course it won't be as it was before. How can it? Those that did not fit are no longer bricks. You've tossed these aside. With these pieces missing from your structure, the paradigm has significantly shifted. The bricks that were once next to the now missing bricks have become stronger. They had to. This that once was your Tower, is now a fortress. It is stronger. It is a worthy encasement for your light, your star.

Be mindful that if a piece does not fit, do not try to force it in. You are only building another Tower if you do. Every Tower represents a lesson that you have to go back and try again to learn. The quicker you learn, the sooner you can move on and put your energy into new growth instead of repeating the same old thing over and over again. How many Towers will it take for you to learn a lesson? Life is precious. How much of it will be devoted to learning the same lesson? Face it, learn from it, move on from it.

Whatever pain you find yourself in during upheavals in your life, be sure to heal them. Don't leave any hurt unattended to. Neglected pain has an irritating way of reappearing at inopportune times. Finding the strength and the courage to face any pain in the here and now will prevent even greater pain later.

It can happen in a Tower Incident that a portion of your soul becomes fragmented and buried beneath the rubble. When you face something so traumatic and hurtful that facing it head on is too painful in the moment, you shut the piece of your self off that feels it the most rather than to feel the pain of the situation. While this may be beneficial to our immediate sanity, it is detrimental to our overall wellbeing.

When you are not whole, you cannot experience life as fully as possible. Remember, happiness is your absolute birthright. To be whole is to be happy. The fragmentation of your soul will have a ripple effect, emanating outward to almost every aspect of your life.

Consider your soul, your authentic self as a mirror in which your truth is reflected. If there is a piece of that mirror missing, your reflection will be incomplete. How can you see the truth of who you are? How can others? There is a distortion in the reflection of their self that they see reflected in you. You will feel incomplete. It will feel as if there is hole in your heart, and of course, there will be.

It is a good idea not to leave the scene of a fallen Tower until all the debris has been sifted through to make sure you walk away complete and whole. Leave no portion of your soul behind. To do so will only cause difficulties for yourself later on. Pull yourself together now. Keep yourself strong, keep yourself whole, keep yourself healed.

Maybe you do not integrate a fragment of yourself in the time and the place where you pick it up. Maybe you pick it up, hold on to it and integrate it later in another place and time. Perhaps you have the piece, but you still need to pick up other pieces so this piece will fit. Maybe these have been lost in the debris of long ago fallen Towers like the piece of a jigsaw puzzle. It's one thing to have in your hand one piece out of a thousand, but unless you have the pieces that it fits into, it's just a piece of a puzzle. It hardly presents the entire picture. But it will. It will when the other pieces are in place.

Maybe you are still looking for these pieces. Sometimes the pieces get lost. It happens. A piece of our self can be lost beneath the rubble of some lost Tower from long ago, maybe even from another lifetime. These pieces may become shadows and can be sought after by following the shadow back to the light, as discussed with the Devil. Follow the shadow back to the light to find the original source of it. Once found, do what you can to heal it. Send your past self healing energy.

If you are attuned to Reiki, meditate and draw the power symbol and the distance symbol. Visualize yourself in the turbulent time. See yourself, even standing over the you of then, giving a hands-on treatment.

If you are not sure when the dark time was, if you ponder that maybe it was a childhood trauma beyond the scope of your memory, simply visualize yourself as a child. Find your inner child. Send Reiki to this past version of you.

If you are not attuned to Reiki, you can still do this. With or without the Reiki symbols, you can send love and light to your past self. Simply follow the steps above , minus the symbols, and send healing light. Green or pink is a good color light to send for love. Gold is good color for healing. White is a good color for spiritual advancement. Visualize these colors. Allow your past self to absorb them.

Sending healing to your past self is one of the greatest acts of love and compassion you can do for yourself. There will be moments that your past self will have unexplained moments of bliss. These will be felt as divine gifts, a moment of rest in the otherwise turbulent journey of chaos.

Your past self may ask, "Where did that feeling come from?" You may not have an answer for where it came from, but you will certainly appreciate it. It may not be in your awareness yet to give thanks to the universe just yet for such things, but the universe knows your gratitude. Your past self will thank you. Your present self will feel the gratitude.

How do you avoid building new towers? This is simple. Listen to your gut. What are your instincts telling you? Activate your inner High Priestess. Let her guide you. Take what she tells you to your inner Emperor. Let him help you formulate a plan and stick to that plan. Tap into your Strength and don't let yourself be bowled over by the life or the demands of other people who will drag you down and build a Tower for you brick by brick by brick. Listen to your gut and follow it. Your gut will keep you free from the Tower.

The Tower Point

No Fool becomes Enlightened without first making his way through the Tower. Remember that spark, that divine light that is within you? Remember how it becomes imprisoned within a cell of cinder-blocks and wants to be free, to shine? Well, The Tower gives it its chance.

At the Tower, that light will stay contained no longer. It will burst free and shine in all its glory. Something must initiate this liberation. Something must trigger the revelation that you are living a lie. The life you are living is not the life you intended for yourself. Something must, like a lightning bolt, strike you and wake you up to this. What will this be?

By the nature of the Tower, this will be something dramatic. The death of a loved one may force you to examine your life from another angle. The loss of a job and financial security may demand that you reconsider what is important and what is not important. A divorce, natural disaster, loss of home, court case, bad neighbor, failing grade, birth of a baby, car accident, demotion, disease… the list is endless. Whatever the mechanism of instigation may be, it is important for your own Enlightenment that you accept it for what it is and allow yourself to be awakened by it.

Consider it this way. You journey forth in life with a misconceived idea about who you are. You think you are one thing, when really, you are another. An enlightened life can be seen as divided in two phases. Phase one- when you "think" you know what life is all about. This is before The Tower, before the lightning bolt. Phase two- when you "know" what life is all about, when your Tower has been struck and your light is set free. Here, you have an epiphany, or perhaps a series of epiphanies that jolt you to a higher understanding of yourself.

What are some examples of this? For starters, let's consider job security and financial status. It is so easy to get caught up in the mindset that more money equals better living, a bigger house means happier times, a nicer car creates a better self-image. Okay. Great. But what happens if you lose your job? What do you do now that you can't afford that big house or that nice car? Is life over? Are you no longer whole? Did you lose your viability as a human being?

Maybe your spouse unexpectedly leaves you. This doesn't kill you, does it? Sure, it hurts, but take a deep breath. Did you notice that? Your lungs still work. Good. Keep breathing and accept the changes that this new situation presents. Your life has changed, but it is not over. Brace yourself for a new adventure. You might actually like it. In time, you probably will.

You do of course, have free will in your life. This means to meet these challenges is to decide how to handle them. You can face them, or you can shirk away from them. To shirk away from them is to deny yourself the opportunity to learn the lesson you had planned to learn from it. These lessons, placed on your path by your guides by way of synchronicity must now be recreated to have another chance to learn this lesson.

Take a look at your life. It didn't end because of these challenges. Sure, it shifted a bit; you had to make some changes, probably even some sacrifices, but so what! Embrace the new paradigm! Maybe now you are forced to look for a new start somewhere completely different. Awesome!

It could be that for your highest and best good to be attained, this new beginning was necessary. Synchronicities lined up to make it happen. Thank your team of divine helpers, because now you are living a fuller life. In these changes, the true you emerges. Changes lead to new ideas, new mind-sets, and new attitudes. Allow these for yourself. Don't put up resistance to them. Your true light is shining. This is your awakening.

Some people will hear the call to awaken, but they do not do so. They do not do so out of fear- fear that what they have built in this lifetime will crumble. What they are not realizing is that these things must crumble. They serve no higher purpose than simple ego gratification. These things that they built are mere symbols of the "I" ego. Things built to say, "Look at me!" But the "me" they are referring to is a false "me." It is a "me" based on social conditioning, not based on the plan created for this lifetime.

What you do not achieve this lifetime will be given another chance in another lifetime. How many lifetimes will it take? The universe has infinite patience with you in this, knowing the challenges involved with, when incarnated on the earth, hearing the voices and awakening to and accepting your purpose. Consider though, accepting life lessons and moving beyond the Tower Point opens you to new growth and new horizons. Why not face what you must face and move beyond it? Why not position yourself that much closer to true Enlightenment?

Our spirits are our spirits, and the truth of who we are with or without our earthly bodies. Therefore, while we inhabit our earthly bodies, the material possessions, relationships, and status we pick up are meaningless. They serve only to comfort us for a short time. So that which you pick up, be willing to let it go when it no longer serves you. It is true that our earthly bodies do need material belongings to survive, and while some things may not be necessary for survival, they do bring us happiness, and happiness is our birthright. The true trick is to accept what you don't need, what you are carrying as extra weight, and let go of it. Keep your load light. The lighter the load, the less debris at The Tower Point.

To put it simply, you reach The Tower Point when you realize and accept that your life thus far has been a lie. Perhaps you have not realized that your life has been a lie. Perhaps you have been living under a false understanding. You have built your life around a paradigm that has nothing to do with your truth. You have not opened your eyes yet to such concepts, so you don't know any better. Your life is driven by your ego, and the life you have built for yourself stands on this foundation.

But the time comes when you awaken. You sense the falseness that so far has been your life. How do you react? Do you accept it or resist it? It's natural to resist, because it is so foreign and strange at first. But your team will not simply give up. They will continue to try and awaken you until you finally listen and realize your true highest and best good.

Not everybody will listen in their current life time. They continue to resist and experience their falling Tower again and again, likely driving themselves crazy and those around them crazy as well trying to find and place blame for the perceived terrible conditions of their lives. They do not realize that to accept the lie as a lie is to be set free of the lie. Acceptance allows the debris of the fallen tower to be swept away, allowing the true self to shine.

The Universe will keep putting you back at The Tower Point until you finally accept it for what it is, embrace it and open to the benefit it has for you. There are multitudes of benefits to be enjoyed at The Tower Point. See them! Open to them! Know that they are there even if they seem to be invisible. This invisibility is just the ego blinding you to them. Remove the blinders of the ego and experience life to the fullest! See reality for the first time. Experience the truth of what life is, what you are. Do not let the ego ruin this for you.

To get successfully from phase one of life to phase two means to have a successful Tower Experience. To be Enlightened, you must have a Tower Experience. We must reach The Tower Point and summon the courage to get through it without retreating out of fear. You must.

It is easy to back out of The Tower Point. What is behind us, while maybe not happiness, is at least familiar, and familiarity can be comforting. What is ahead is a new world. You must find the strength and the courage to allow your Tower to crumble, fall, and become completely demolished. You must not retreat from it. You must face it. You must stare down and push past what you see of your self when the falsehood of your misconceptions are revealed.

To evolve is to reach the Tower Point and then go beyond it, to leave the rubble of the Tower behind. Personal evolution is enlightenment. Enlightenment is to have your light liberated from its prison cell atop the tower and finally allow it to shine freely. When your light is liberated, allow it to shine. Don't rebuild the tower. Why put your light back in its cell?

Perhaps in your light, others will find the courage to move beyond their own stagnation and to liberate their own light from their cells atop their own Towers, and in turn will coax their light to a flame to an inferno. In this way, we all evolve. We evolve as individuals as well as a species.

Evolving as individuals has the benefit of expanding consciousness. We become aware of the perfection and the beauty in many things. Expand that to the evolution of the entire species where each individual member of the species wakes up to their own perfection.

Imagine that everybody realizes their own perfection and own inspirations and pursue these without the distractions that others dump on them. Imagine the perfection of the world if everybody would simply get out of their head and into their heart and accept what they find at the Tower Point. This is the evolution of the human species. It is what we are headed towards. As we move beyond our personal Towers, we perfect ourselves. As we perfect ourselves, we perfect the species. As we perfect the species, the planet becomes a better place to be because it is now inhabited by enlightened beings living their truth with the rubble of their lies behind them. That's what it takes to for the species to evolve. It really is that simple.

Ask Yourself:

- Can I admit when I am wrong?
- Do I have a victim mentality, or can I see the big picture when something doesn't go my way?
- Do I learn, or do I make the same mistake over and over?
- Do I make excuses?
- Do I feel whole? If not, what is missing?

The Star
17

Key Words

Talents
Liberation
Purity
Shining
Authenticity

When you are doing what you love, you shine. You are on the road to Enlightenment. What are your real true talents? What represents bliss to you? What sets you apart from others? What are you admired for?

That light within you, that spark that was locked away in the Tower has now been liberated. It is set free to shine. Your authentic self is now let loose. Are you ready to follow your own true real passions?

This spark is your truest, most honest, purest self. This is the self that is unaffected by social conditioning and expectations. This self is represented by your talents and your ambitions. It is represented by your unique contributions and perspective of the world and the universe.

You come to the earth wanting to shine this light. To radiate. You want to shine forth this truth of yourself so that the world may benefit from your unique wisdom and knowings.

Sometimes you put up blocks to this light that prevent it from shining outward to the world. These blocks come about in the form of limiting beliefs, social conditioning, ego, worry, sadness and fear.

Fear of what? Fear that your true self may not be acceptable to others. That others may perceive you as "weird" or "strange" for being who you really are. We become so accustomed to "fitting in" and "conforming" to our social groups and to the larger essence of our society that it is easy to forget our unique qualities. When this happens, our Star Quality lays dormant. It's still there. It hasn't died. It is simply asleep.

It is time to embrace your truth and wake up your Star Quality. It is time to shine. Let the blocks crumble. Encourage them to. Make them. Ask for help in this crumbling. Invoke your spirit guides, your angels. Invoke Jesus, Buddha, Lord Ganesh, or whoever is meaningful to you in such an endeavor.

It is important to bear in mind that you are not alone. You have an incredible team of spirits and angels who are willing, able, and desiring to help you on your way. They are, in fact, helping you with or without your conscience awareness of their presence. They do not do it for personal glory. They are not motivated by ego. They do it because they want you to experience your incarnation on the earth as richly and fully as you can.

It can take courage to be our true authentic self. You must encourage others to be their self as well, to truly shine as they are meant to shine, for when one is shining as they are meant to shine, they truly brighten and even change the world. It is your talents and your thoughts that others pick up on and add their own knowings and understandings to. In so doing, we continue to generate more and more understandings and knowings, both within ourselves and within others. So, it is very important to remove blocks and allow our Star energy to fill the world. We all possess something of value. We must let our Star Qualities shine.

When you are doing what you love, you shine. You are truly in the flow. Your creative energy flows effortlessly. Your brain takes a break, and you simply surrender to the process and allow your spirit to take over. This always feels good. When you create this way, you just know that you are achieving your highest and greatest good. Ask yourself, what puts you into this state? What are you doing when you put your thoughts on the back burner and go with the flow of your inner creator? This is your true talent, your Star Quality.

When you discover it, utilize it. Make time for it. Not only does this create a positive feeling within you, the world also benefits from your creative output. Explore this. Ask yourself, "What makes me a Star?" When you are following your bliss, you shine. When you shine, you generate gravity. When you generate gravity, the right people are drawn to you. So shine! Live your passion! Draw to you, the people whose energy you can create dynamic synergies with.

Do not fight your true nature. If you are an artist, be an artist. If you are a poet, be a poet. If you are a compassionate being, be compassionate. If you hate loud music, don't pretend to like it. If you love classical music, then love it with all you have even if those around you can't stand it. Be true. Be authentic. Do not wall yourself in. As long as you fight your Star Quality, as long as you struggle against your reality, the more you will suffer. This suffering is pointless.

Accepting yourself as yourself is the beginning of personal evolution. Personal evolution is the beginning of species evolution because the species as a whole will only evolve when the individual members of the species evolve themselves. How can you evolve if you are not authentic? Living authentically will generate one synchronicity after another after another after another that will lead you to the highest pinnacle of your existence. By denying your authentic self, you will only deny the opportunities to experience these synchronicities. Why do that?

Be authentic and evolve! Let your Star Quality shine as brightly and intensely as it was always meant to. This is your birthright. Enjoy it.

Ask Yourself:

- What are my talents?
- What makes me shine?
- What about me attracts others?
- Do I fear success?
- What do I love to do?

The Moon

18

Key Words

Mystery
Subtext
Doubt
Patience
Surreal

Things seem different in the light of the moon. Be careful believing what you see in moon shadows. Be patient and wait for the sun to rise before accepting anything you see.

The Moon tells us that things seem a certain way. But are they really? Moon energy can manifest in our lives in a number of ways. The Moon invites us to ask, "What is really going on? What is happening below the surface? What is not seen? What is being withheld from me?" It is a good idea to investigate all the details before making a final decision or signing any contracts. A classic example of this involves buying a car. Would you not take the car for a test drive before buying it? Shouldn't you have a trusted mechanic look it over to make sure it all checks out before forking over your money for it? Don't rush into anything without knowing all the details first.

It is normal to feel worry and to feel stress. We all do at one time or another. The important thing is to not let it control you. Moon energy can do that to you- it can make you doubt the most basic things you know of yourself and the world. It simply casts a very different shadow on your inner landscape that makes everything look so strange and different, for a time.

Things are very different in the light of the moon. When your mind is fixated on the doom and the gloom, you see only the darkness. Be careful of the decisions you make under the influence of The Moon, for once the Moon passes and the sun shines again, you will see illumination in those Moon Shadows.

Do you sometimes try to fall asleep while something weighs heavily on your mind? Chances are, while you lie awake with this stress you can conceive a multitude of horrible scenarios. You may swear that you will take a most drastic measure in reaction to it. Then you finally drift off to sleep, even if only for a couple of hours. When you wake up after these couple of hours, the worry and stress does not seem so relevant anymore. The Moon has released its hold on you.

Eventually the sun rises and you see things in a more "real" setting. It is best to wait out these Moon Shadows before reacting to what you find in them. Let the sun rise above the horizon before judging what you see. Always be mindful of these Moon Shadows. That fear, that worry, that stress you feel that keeps you from sleeping, these are demons of the Moon Shadows. They may only be conjured by your imagination, but they are very real. To react to them without first shining light onto them can be costly. When you react to a problem that is not real, you may only be creating problems that were not there to begin with. Now you have a real problem to deal with.

When you feel lost in the shadow of the Moon, be prepared to examine the tiny details of a situation. Is everything as it seems? Is everything as you hope it to be? Do you know what you are getting yourself into? Should you be doing something differently? Double check everything. Re-examine all the facts, attitudes, feelings, ideas, worries, stresses. Have patience and take the time to do this. It can only save you troubles in the time ahead.

Ask Yourself:

- How well do I handle worry and stress?
- Do I react impulsively to a situation, or do I wait for clarity?
- Do I examine the details of a situation closely enough?
- Am I patient?
- When examining a situation, am I missing anything?

The Sun

19

Key Words

Good Vibes
Happiness
Good Times
The Right Place
Energized

When you are in the right place doing the right thing, you just know it. You feel good inside, and this radiates outwards to the outer you. Everything feels right, because it is right.

Sometimes you will find yourself in such and such a place that brings out the best of who you are. This is a place of harmony and positive energy. This energy emanates both from the earth itself and the people around you. There is something from this energy that you are meant to receive. As you soak this energy in, you are made strong. You are uplifted. This is the energy of the Sun.

The Sun is a star that generates gravity. Think of it this way. Think of the sun as that which keeps you grounded. There is not a sense of "I got to get out of here." There is a sense of rooting in. There is a sense of contentment. There is a sense that there is no other place to be than right here, right now. You have found a gravitational pull that is compatible with you. It keeps you grounded right where you want to be.

There are countless examples of one's personal Sun. It could be just the right university. It could be the right town, job, company, coffee shop, beach, or something as broad as an entire country or continent. Maybe it is a vacation spot. Maybe it is a place to live. Maybe it is the perfect street to go for walks on. Where are you when you feel the best? What are you getting out of this spot? This is your personal Sun energy. You have found your Sun and you are basking in it. The gravity of this is perfectly suited for you. Enjoy it.

When you are grounded, you have found yourself in the place where you are receiving what you truly need from your earthly experience. So many people seek this. Achieving it is doable, but not everybody is fully able to. Some are where they most beneficially belong, but do not open their awareness to it. This is unfortunate, for to understand and realize that you are in the gravitational pull of your Sun is to fully benefit from what the earth has to offer you, right where you are. So ask yourself, what is it about this spot that you love so much? What about this place makes you feel good?

The Sun feels good. Think about this. After a long rain, doesn't it feel nice when the sun finally comes back out? When it is dreary and overcast, don't you patiently wait for the clouds to clear to see and feel the sun again? When you are cooped up in an office, don't you like to step outside, if only for a few minutes to feel the sun on your face? Doesn't this make you feel better? In this way, the Sun is a healing force. Tap into this. What can you do to energetically heal yourself and make yourself feel better? What can you do to put yourself in a better mood?

Tap into your inner Sun. In it is clarity, healing energy, and simple good vibes. You are entitled to these things. We all are. Enjoy them and feel good.

Ask Yourself:

- Where am I and what am I doing when I feel the best about myself?
- When I feel down, what usually makes me feel better?
- What places and activities am I naturally drawn to?
- Do I feel grounded?
- What heals me?

Awakening

20

Key Words

Your Calling
Waking Up
Destiny
Assessment
Spirals

When you hear the call to wake up, pay attention! You are being summoned by much higher forces than your mere mind. These sources know who and what you are destined to become. Listen to them. Make the choice to become the best version of yourself. Move forward. Do not backtrack.

You live in pseudo-lightness until you successfully get through the Tower Point. On the other side of The Tower, the landscape is different. You will see things you did not see before. Your perception is now attuned to it. The filters of ego, social conditioning, and expectations are removed. These filters get left behind at the Tower Point and a new perspective is now presented. This perspective is the truth. It can be startling and foreign at first, but to embrace it ushers in a new era of harmony for anybody who is open to it. Are you ready to embrace it? You have reached the point of Judgment, and you are being asked.

You have gotten through the Tower Point successfully at last. Now, do you heed the call of your authentic self? Do you accept it? What do you do? Do you embrace your destiny? Are you ready to be this new entity? Or do you resist? How long will you resist? Will you rise from the grave of stagnation and ascend to the level of your true greatness, or will you stay as you are, smaller than you are meant to be?

In many ways, Awakening is a spiritual assessment. It may or not be perceived on the level of the conscious self. It is to be experienced more than it is to be intellectualized about. It is a product of faith. Awakening and faith go hand in hand. Have faith that what is in your highest and best interest is being provided. Have faith that the true self you found liberated at the Tower really is your true-true self.

This trust and faith is your wake up call. The trick is to hear it and pay attention to it. Those that do prosper. Those that don't… well, let's not say that they suffer, but they do miss out on some pretty great things in life.

Those that don't tend to spin around in the same little circles worrying about the same little problems and making the same, same, same, complaints. Waking up means instead of spinning around in circles, how about expanding outward? How about creating a spiral? How about as you see the same starting point coming up again, you expand outward instead of meeting it again? How about growing? How about considering and pondering the lessons that you learned on the way around and using it as strength to go beyond your previous ideas of limits and boundaries? How about taking an honest look at what you cling to that serves no purpose?

Pay attention! Look at what the patterns you repeat bring to your life.

Realize when you must make a change. Think change is scary? Try staying exactly the same your whole life. Now that's a scary thought! To never change, to repeat the same patterns over and over again means to never grow and to never evolve. If you are not evolving as an individual, how is the species supposed to? Evolution is a group endeavor. We are all in this together. Get on board and make the necessary changes to your life to make it happen. Let go of addictions and detrimental patterns. Release limiting thoughts. Set free the social conditioning that says you can only be what you currently are.

Can human kind evolve to its next level of existence as long as so many cling to old ideas and addictions? Old ideas may have served their purpose in their time, but that was a different time. Now you are living in the now-this now. Honor those old ideas by setting them free. Embrace the ideas that serve you in the current now. And what is an addiction but a fear of letting go? What is it but a fear that by letting go, a gap will be formed that you are unsure of what will fill it?

As humans, we love our paradigms. One of our greatest fears is the shifting of one. Is this not true? Think about it. We get into our routines. We get used to them. We get upset when our routines are disrupted. This includes addictions. Whether they are healthy or not, to deviate from the pattern set by an addiction creates a feeling of disconnect. This disconnect manifests as fear. What will fill in the gap left by this disconnection?

Addictions can also validate our pursuits. "I can accomplish such and such as long as I (fill in addiction)." "(Fill in addiction) gives me the power to (fill in the blank)." To release the addiction would mean having to prove our self without it. Our minds work such that we love to attach an effect to a cause. By attaching the perceived effect of an addiction to the cause, we only deny ourselves of our true talents. Our talents are our divinity. To attach the effect to the cause of the addiction is to deny our own divinity, or to undermine it significantly. So, can humanity evolve while clinging to addictions and using them as excuses and validation?

To wake up and to appreciate your purpose in life is to laugh at your addictions and the validation you find in them. To wake up is to let go of your addictions and prove your greatness without them.

How will you react to life beyond the Tower Point? Will you forge ahead,

111

break new ground, reach new horizons, surmount obstacles, and explore new plateaus? Or will you retreat to your old ways? Cling to old habits? You do of course, have free will. You are absolutely entitled to do as you please. Just keep in mind, you now know yourself. Your truth has been presented to you. You now have a chance at an authentic life. You might as well go for it.

Ask Yourself:

- Do I repeat the same patterns that keep me stuck?
- Do I fear change?
- Am I being completely honest with myself?
- Do I see myself as unlimited?
- Do I want to make changes to better my life?

The World

21

Key Words

Success
Finality
Achievement
Full Circle
Arrival

The return home is never the same after a Fool's journey, because the Fool is different. No longer young and naive, the Fool is full with the wisdom and the knowings of the journey. This shifts his perspective and alters his wisdom. What is familiar to him, he may now have a new appreciation for, or perhaps disdain for. Returning home is an opportunity for the Fool to gauge who he has become.

If you view life as a journey, if the purpose of life is to learn and to grow, if you look at life as a series of destinations and plateaus to be reached, then the World is the destination. Once you reach this destination, what happens? Does this mean your life is over? Hardly. It simply means that you made it successfully through the Tower Point. You shed your old skin and grew into something new. You put behind you the old ways and the old thought patterns that were holding you back. It means you have become this new, better being and as such, you are now ready to face the world with a fresh perspective and a new set of eyes. You have actuated yourself to living an authentic life. You have acclimated yourself to your true truth and now, you are living it. This was no small achievement.

Your goals have been achieved. Pat yourself on the back and reflect on the journey. Go over the ups and downs and the highs and the lows. What brought you to this point in life? Sometimes it was easy and sometimes it was difficult. Sometimes the lessons were obvious, other times not. Be that as it may be though, they are what brought you to where you are so it was all good.

You search. You know you are meant for something. Sometimes though, you ask, "What exactly would that be? What exactly am I meant for?" And so you seek an answer to this very profound yet basic question. You try things. You examine things. You figure out what exactly feels right to you and then you compare. You decide what is truly meaningful and important to you. If you are wise, you realize the answer and latch onto it. You nurture it. You make it grow. This feels right to you. This is your purpose. This is a big reason why you are here. Pay attention to this. What in your life truly feels right and perfect?

There is satisfaction in achieving a goal. These goals are not arbitrary. They do, in so many ways, define who you are. These goals are your passions. They exist in your heart. They are attached to your soul. You dedicate yourself to them. You strive and work for them. And then... at last... you achieve it. It is an accumulation of effort and simple dedication. Now, you can enjoy the results of these efforts. Now you have shifted your own personal paradigm. Now, you are not defined as somebody "trying" but as somebody who has "achieved." This achievement gives you a new sense of solid ground to stand on. You now have a firm foundation. From this new plateau, where will you go now? Based on your successes, what is next?

You are ready for the next journey. It is time to take the success, wisdom, and knowledge you have amassed and go in a new direction with it. Considered sequentially, it is time to begin again at zero. It is time to be a Fool again. You are stronger, wiser and more powerful. Your leaps of faith are more calculated and thought through now. What direction does our heart tell you to go now? It is time to listen and to follow.

Again.

Ask Yourself:

- Have I arrived?
- How have I changed over time?
- Do I truly appreciate life?
- Have I reached my goals?
- What's next?

The Minor Arcana

The minor arcana represents our shared experience of being present on the planet. It creates a road map of our personal journey as we navigate the plateaus of earthly existence. What does it mean to be in human form? What experiences do we all share and give a name to?

What desires, fears, needs, joys, sorrows, worries, frustrations, elations, happinesses, ups and downs do we all experience? How well have you personally mastered each? Which truly resonate with you? Which would you like to develop? Which scare you? Which entice you? Which come easy to you? Which are challenging?

The minor arcana is divided into four aspects of earthly life, with fourteen cards devoted to each. These four aspects are the human qualities of Passions, Desires, Speculation, and Creation.

Passions: This is your fire energy. What do you get excited about? What are you dreams, hopes, and ambitions? What energy do you put into achieving these?

Desires: This is your emotional energy. What turns you on? What turns you off? How well do you handle your emotions? How well do you express them? How receptive are you?

Speculation: This is your mental energy. How in control are you of your thoughts? What effect do your thoughts have on you? Are you able to harness the power of your thoughts, or do they bowl you over?

Creation: This is your material energy, and your connection to the earth. How well are your personal needs being met? How well do you utilize the resources at your disposal? Do you give as well as take? Do you have an earthly consciousness?

Passions: <u>WANDS</u> *Fire Energy*

Ace of Passions

Imagine the initial spark of inspiration. You have a great idea. This spark is worth becoming a fire. Feed this spark. Give it what it needs to grow. Keep feeding it until it is an inferno.

This is how simple ideas become powerful institutions. They are not forgotten or dismissed. Pay attention to the inspirations that come your way. Bring them to life. Have patience with them as they ascend to greatness. Feed them, nurture them, and watch them grow. You have the ability to be a powerful creator. Tap into that power.

Now that you have new ideas and a new drive to succeed, will you act on it? These inspirations you have received are worth something. They most certainly are not for nothing, and they did not arbitrarily come to you. These inspirations are your gift from the universe. Utilize them! Activate their power! Follow these inspirations to success!

Two of Passions

You have the whole world in your hands. You can do anything you want with it. So, the question is, what will you do with it? Will you do great things? Will you utilize it to your greatest potential? Or will you set it down and forget about it? Will it become a ghost of the dream that it could have, should have, been?

By appreciating what you have at your disposal, the world is yours. Be neglectful and squander the gifts of inspiration you are given, and it will be increasingly difficult to find more ideas and new inspirations. Why make it difficult for yourself? Appreciating what you have makes life that much easier.

The choice is yours. You can either utilize what you have at your disposal or let it slip away. In this, you must find balance between your will to achieve and succeed with your desire to put in the effort. It is, after all, all about effort. Those that infuse their opportunities with necessary effort will achieve great things. Those that do not will sit around wondering why they are unhappy and not getting what they want out of life.

Three of Passions

What lies beyond the horizon? That place you have not yet been? Are you adventurous enough to explore? Are you willing to leave behind that which is safe and secure to see what is there? This, of course

can easily be metaphorical. Are you limiting your potential by enforcing limiting beliefs? What is it that you are telling yourself that you cannot do? Why are you telling yourself these things? Do you think you know yourself that well?

Perhaps what you believe of yourself is what the ego tells you. The ego has some pretty strong ideas about what the body can, and more significantly, cannot do. But what is your heart telling you? It knows a much more intrinsic truth. It knows your true limits, which in all actuality, do not exist. When your mind tells you otherwise, laugh at it. Find humor in the assertions of the ego that you cannot do this or do that, and prove it wrong. Go beyond your "limits." Get out of the box. Whatever "it" is, do it.

Why limit yourself to what is familiar? There are so many horizons and so many opportunities. Doesn't life become stagnant and boring if you don't challenge yourself? Be bold! Be adventurous! Don't just stare at pictures of a faraway land. Don't just think about it. See it with your own eyes! Enrich yourself! Expand yourself! Make no excuses why you cannot! You can! The time for action is now, so do it!

Four of Passions

It is a good feeling to be excited. The feeling of excitement is a strong indicator that you are on the right track. Your gut is screaming "Yes!" Excitement is an awesome motivator. When you know that what you are

embarking on is the most perfect thing in the moment for you, how can you not want to do nothing but that? Your ambitions are validated and you have fuel for the Chariot. It is a great affirmation from within.

With excitement, things seem to fall into place. It seems like whatever you need to accomplish a goal magically appears. This is because this feeling of being fired up, being charged with enthusiasm is a powerful indicator to the powers that be of the universe that you want what you want. Now, with the energy of creation and raw power surging through you outward to the cosmos, what you need is naturally drawn to you. The best way to accomplish anything is to be excited about it.

Do not dismiss excitement. When considering an idea, look to your gut feelings about it. Does it just flop around like a dying fish? If so, it may not be the best idea to pursue. Obviously, you do not have a passion for it. Without a passion for it, how much of your energy are you going to put into it? Without your energy, how will it ever become what you want it to become?

Or does it take off like a rocket? This is a good idea! This is something you can willfully devote your time and energy to! Why hold back? Go for it!

Five of Passions

Have you become complacent? Have you gotten too relaxed in your comfort zone? Have you reached a point where you know you can rest with your accomplishments? Well guess what? Something or some-

body will inevitably come along to challenge your perceptions of what your personal best is. It is called competition, and its purpose is to expand your thoughts about what you are and what you can do.

To be challenged is to find new routes to perfection and to realign your thoughts about how good you actually are. It is to reassess your limits and to redefine what it means to be on top. When faced with competition, you must tap into your personal drive to stay on top. Without competition, without having another to gauge your standing against, you may never aim to be better.

Look to those who have similar ambitions. Look to those who are working to achieve the same that you are working to achieve. Where do you consider yourself in relation to them? This competition need not be cutthroat. It is not even necessary for this other person to even know you consider them competition. If it helps the both of you strive for perfection, its fine, but for your own purposes, it is not necessary. Just watch them and strive to be better. It's a good way to become your best.

Six of Passions

Congratulations. You followed your impulses and your brilliance, and now your ideas have paid off. You didn't listen to anybody (external or internal) who told you what you cannot or should not do. You listened

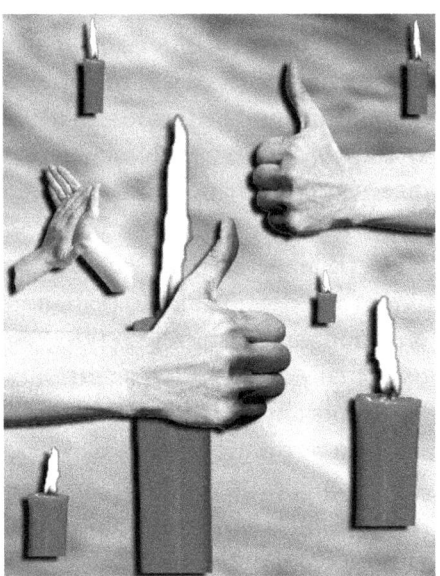

to your own inner-guidance system and it has led you to a very good place, and others have noticed.

Accept praise. You don't have to be humble. These people praising you are your supporters. They are your cheerleaders. They believe in what you are capable of, and they want to see you do it. So do it! Do it for them! Show them that the faith they have in you is well placed. Do it for yourself to prove to yourself that you can do anything.

Reflect on your accomplishments. Appreciate what you have done. And how about others? How are they doing? Have you said congratulations to a colleague for their achievements? Don't hold back on that. Let them know their work is noticed and appreciated. Just as you will appreciate this, so will they. Be a supporter. Be a cheerleader. Sometimes knowing that they have your support can make a difference to somebody doing their best to get something done.

Seven of Passions

Do you ever feel stuck? Like you have gone as far as you can go, even though you really want to go a whole lot farther? We all have moments like that. Take a deep breath. Relax. Now take a step back. Take

in the situation from a broader perspective. What got you to this moment of stuckedness has been a narrow view.

What else do you see in the fringes of your perspective? What do you see right outside? This is where the solution is. It is where you haven't thought to look yet. "Yet" is the most important word here. It is not that you never would look here, it is just that thus far, it has not occurred to you to do so. And why is this?

This is because you were confident enough in your narrow view. It doesn't mean that your narrow view was wrong, it just is not what you need right now. Right now, you need a broad perspective.

You were sure the solution would be right in front of you. It is not until now that you realize that, no. It isn't. It is necessary to look outside of your perception for it. Do this and you will see a broader range of solutions. Now that you see broader solutions, you can proceed.

Imagine your quandary as a wall. If you can't go over it, go under it. If you can't go under it, go around it. If you can't go around it, bust it down and go through it. Most importantly, don't just stand there staring at it. You have the power to get to the other side. Find it.

Eight of Passions

The world is waiting… for you. The synchronicities have lined up. The doors have opened. The opportunities are at hand. What is required now? For you to do your part. And you know what your part is. Whatever

that may be- you know what it is, and now is the time to do it! Success is nigh. Make the effort now that you need to make, and you will benefit from it greatly. Do it.

If you didn't do it yesterday, don't worry about it. But don't wait for tomorrow. Now- right now is the best time. You've been inspired. You have the resources. You have the support. What are you waiting for? Do it!

A window of opportunity has opened for you. This window is support, motivation, enthusiasm, and pure and simple willpower. Strike while the iron is hot! What happens when it cools off? What happens when the enthusiasm dies down? What happens when the support you have steps away because you're not actually doing what you say you will do? Then the burden is to get it hot again. Why spend energy this way? Why not jump in and do it now? Why let it cool down in the first place?

Nine of Passions

L earn what there is to be learned from all of your experiences, both the positive and the negative ones. If something didn't go quite the way you planned and you end up feeling beaten by the world from it, should

you give up? Or should you learn the lesson the experience has to teach and try again? If need be, try again and again and again. It's been said millions of times now, but it is worth repeating here- "What doesn't kill you only makes you stronger." It's a tired and old cliché, but it is also apt advice.

Sometimes in pursuit of your ambitions, you run into obstacles. Your goals are not always achieved easily or overnight. Sometimes they take a great deal of effort, perseverance and strength to bring them to actualization. It is often easy to give up and decide it is just not worth it. When the going gets tough, do you throw in the towel and say "I give up" or do you keep trying, keep reinventing, keep facing the continued obstacles thrown in your path until you finally reach the goal you set out to achieve?

To truly achieve success on the earth, don't run and hide after life punches you in the gut. You know what? Getting punched in the gut by life happens. The powerful among us in their chosen fields are the ones who toughened up from these punches. Your goals are achievable. Success is on the horizon. Just don't give up getting there! Endure whatever hardships may exist on your path, for they are only temporary. They are defeatable. Get past them, get through them, get around them and the world is yours.

Ten of Passions

Sometimes, you carry a heavy load. You take on a lot of responsibilities and ambitions. In these times, it is necessary to set priorities and to reevaluate what you consider important. If you don't, what happens? In-

stead of giving your energy to that which will grow and prosper, you split your energy amongst several entities, never able to devote a full amount to the one or ones that will blossom into something powerful and worthwhile.

When you find yourself carrying a heavy load, pause for a moment and ask, "What am I carrying that is actually important?" Examine what you are doing, what you are trying to do, and what you feel expected to do. See if there is something you can let go of. Is everything you are carrying important? Which are burdens and extra weight? Can you set any of it down? Can you ask for help with any of it? What can you set aside now and come back to later?

Prioritize. Visualize all that you are working on, all that you are carrying as a spark. Of these sparks, which is most likely to become a fire if you pay the proper attention to it? Devote your energy to this one. Coax this spark into a fire. In doing so, the flames will spread to your other sparks, igniting them into fires as well. With enough fires, soon you will have an inferno. Now, you are truly living your passions.

Student of Passions

As a Student of Passions, don't shy away from your natural curiosity. Don't let the world lose its fascinating qualities. However much you learn, find something to spark your interest. Ask "Why?" Ask "How?"

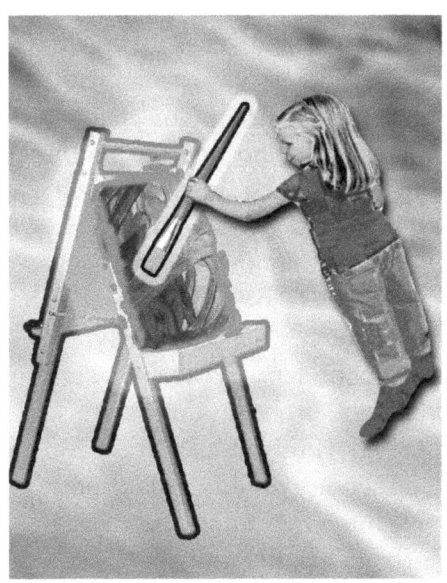

Don't become jaded with the misguided notion that you know it all already.

Latch onto a new idea and study it. Never be afraid to try something new. Always seek that next new thing to be fascinated by. The world is filled with "Wows!" Always be on the lookout for the next one.

What is something you have always been curious about? What is something new that you have wanted to try? What is something you would like to know more about? Indulge it. Try something new. Do something different. Expand your limits just that much more and see what impact it has. Read about something you find interesting. Sign up for a class that you'd like to try. Go for a walk somewhere you have not yet walked. Drive a different route to wherever it is that you are going. Stop and really look at something you have always just walked by.

Are you pursing your own true interests? If you are not, why? Has the world lost its fascination for you? What can you do to regain it? Follow your impulses. Do the things that you find beneficial and interesting. Don't get so lost in the demands of life that you don't seek to enrich your spirit. Always seek to learn a little more... a little more... a little more. The pursuit of new interests opens doors to fascinating other dimensions.

Champion of Passions

As the Champion of Passions, you have confidence, and it seems that things just happen easily for you. When you are positive in your ability to get something done, even the setbacks don't seem so serious. When

you can absolutely visualize the goal you are reaching for, clearly seeing yourself successfully accomplishing it, even the problems you encounter on the way are not so insurmountable. This is to be sure of yourself.

Whether or not things actually do happen easily for you, it certainly looks like they do. This is a byproduct of confidence. When you are confident, problems don't seem so much like problems. With confidence comes assurance that somehow, some way, things are going to work out just fine.

When you are completely sure of yourself, your confidence is palpable. You will radiate with the vibe of success. You will be seen as bold and direct in your decision making. Do not be afraid to fail, for in failure, as you undoubtedly know, there is a lesson to be learned and a clue that points towards ultimate success.

Mother of Passions

As the Mother of Passions, you have talents and skills that enrich your life and the world you live in. Sometimes you will do this in big ways. Sometimes you will do this in small ways. Big ways or small ways- it doesn't matter. It all adds up, as long as you do your part by being active and expressing your talents, however talents such as yours get expressed.

Pursue your talents and your ambitions with full passion. Everybody is a genius in one way or another. In the way that you are a genius, the world benefits. Your genius is illuminated and magnified by those things that you are passionate about. If you have a passion for creating art, give your all to creating art. If you have a passion for playing music, make playing music a priority. If you are brilliant at solving math equations, then make the world that much better a place through solving math equations.

Your talents are your gifts. These gifts both benefit you and the world. Who hasn't been inspired by a great piece of art, a brilliantly written bit of poetry or prose, or an amazing piece of music? Where did these things come from? They came from some talented person who chose to share their talents with the world. Do the same. Share your talents with the world so that somebody somewhere, will be inspired by it.

Father of Passions

As the Father of Passions, you have a natural talent for motivating others. Have you noticed this? Have you noticed you have a certain charisma and charm that makes people want to pay attention to what you

say and follow your lead? This is your Father of Passions quality.

A Father of Passions is a natural leader based on their sincerity and their dedication to their own strength. These are people who know what they are talking about and have generated trust. When you trust somebody, aren't you more likely to appreciate what they say, what they do, and the advice they offer?

As the Father of Passions you see in others their greatest potential. You see this even when they do not see it for their self. You prod and prompt them to come out of their shell, and illuminate their path, showing them what exactly they are capable of.

Those who are truly tuned into their Father of Passions personality tend to be great teachers. They thrive as motivational speakers, life coaches, and in simply giving advice and counsel. They do this through one on one conversation, writing, stage appearances, TV performances, paid counseling, and simple friendship. Perhaps they get their message out via a blog. Maybe Twitter. Perhaps they even do it via a Facebook status. However the means of conveyance, the results are the same. They broadcast their message and are able to inspire others.

As a Father of Passions let there be substance to the words you speak and the messages you convey. Be mindful of who pays attention to you. Your words and your deeds carry more weight than you may realize.

Creation: *Material Energy*
Ace of Creation
PENTACLES

There is an opportunity at hand. The conditions are right for prosperity. What will you do with this opportunity? Will you let it slip away, or will you act on it?

The Ace of Creation is a seed of prosperity. If you plant it and nourish it, what will it grow into? That depends. What does prosperity mean to you? Does it mean material wealth? Does it mean an abundant harvest in the field? Does it mean getting through to students you are trying to teach? Does it mean finding inspiration to write a great novel? Answering this question is an endeavor.

One person cannot possibly answer this with any degree of accuracy for another. What matters is what it means to you. Give this thought, for as you give it thought you generate energy for it. From this energy, your seed of prosperity will grow.

How well are you tending to this seed? Keep your mind free of clutter and focus on it. Distractions are weeds. As your seed grows, keep it free of weeds. Weeds will only choke out what is pure and perfect. Give it attention. Give it energy. Give it light. Examine what is working and what is not. Accentuate what is going well and eliminate what is hindering forward momentum and growth.

From this seed grows your tree of abundance and success. By preparing the soil in which it is planted and by caring for it as it grows, it can grow

132

tall and strong, providing you with prosperity. It is up to you though to see to it that it does. It is up to you to adjust it and reform it as it grows. Once the roots are deeply planted, and it has grown tall, you will appreciate the efforts you put into it.

Two of Creation

You have to do some juggling in life. Sometimes you must juggle time, sometime resources, sometimes finances. It isn't always easy, sometimes you have to do what you have to do.

Imagine using one credit card to pay off another. Did you really get ahead by doing this? No. Not really. All you did was buy yourself another month. The reality is that you will still have to pay off these bills eventually. Sometimes it is a matter of getting by month by month, week by week, day by day, minute by minute. With diligence, you will eventually get ahead. Until then though, keep up the juggling act

Sometimes this may feel like a struggle, other times it can be fun. Do you enjoy the challenge of it? Or do you find it draining of your energy and simply tiresome? If you find this tiresome, what is this telling you? Perhaps it is telling you to finally find a way to break free of this pattern you have set for yourself. Find a solid balance with a secure foundation. If you need resources to break free of the confines of this juggling act, search for it. A new job perhaps. A second job perhaps. Perhaps, tap into your entrepreneurial spirit. What can you create to boost your resources?

Choose to continually juggle, or choose to find a way out of it. By choosing to choose to find a way out, the inspiration you need will find you. By choosing to choose to stay in a rut, the rut will always be there for you. So, what do you choose?

Three of Creation

Sometimes the best way to accomplish something is to do it as a team. Create some synergy, work together, and get it done. Not everything can be accomplished alone. Sometimes you need the help of others. Some-

times others need your help. Sometimes you simply work together to get something done whether or not you even know how your contribution fits into the final outcome. You do it because it is your job. Everybody does their part, and together the job gets done. The spirit of cooperation is fundamental here. Without cooperation, the synergy gets gridlocked. Work together. Cooperate. Accomplish.

Master the art of cooperation. Sometimes you just have to do what is asked of you. Not everything is about you. There will be those times

when you are not the center of attention or the most important person in the room. Sometimes you just have to go along with it. Do your part. Do what is asked of you. Accept your paycheck. Go do your own thing when the day is over. That's how life is sometimes.

Four of Creation

What are you holding onto? What do you have that you could just as easily let go of? By letting go, you create room for new. Accept that which once served you, has since outlived its purpose. Honor this purpose

by releasing it. Life stays fresh this way. Get rid of old items! Take them to a thrift store! Throw them away! It will feel good to relinquish its hold on you and make room for the new. This applies to tangible objects as well as ideas and dogmas. As you let go of these old things, you will find that your mind becomes uncluttered.

Your outer world tends to be a reflection of your inner world. By letting go of the material items you do not need any longer, your thoughts also have a way of becoming less of a burden. Have you noticed this?

When you have just what you need, and just the few things that make you happy, you tend to have a much greater clarity of thought. Try it and see. You will notice that your thoughts and your beliefs become less limited as they are no longer attached to outdated objects and ideas.

Ask yourself, "What am I clinging to? What outdated concepts can I change? What can I let go of? What is absolutely important, and what is ready to be set free?" When you have the answer, act on it. Get rid of those material possessions that you never use and don't need, and meditate the old ideas away. Say to them, "Thank you for serving your purpose in my life, but it is now time for you to go." Then release them.

Five of Creation

Poverty can be either a mindset or physical condition. On the one hand, yes, poverty represents destitution and unfortunate circumstances. This is fact of life for some people. On the other hand though, it can

represent a "poor me" mentality. Some people, maybe a little spoiled, maybe used to getting their own way, maybe used to people catering to them suddenly find they do not have everything they want. They do not have people lining up to help them, and now they must do for themselves. This causes distress. This distress can lead to feelings of uneasiness and maybe even panic.

Because they do not have everything they think they need, they feel like they have nothing. This of course is just a mindset, a mentality. It can be insulting to those people who actually are in need. These "poor me" people really would do well to reevaluate their circumstances and realize that their life is not as bad as they think it is. They should work harder at appreciating what life has given them. They should try to step outside of their self and see how others perceive them. They need to realize that the rest of the world is not here to cater to them. We all have our own problems. They need to develop an awareness of this fact, and if they cannot, they need to accept feeling poor then. This is all a mentality.

Are you willing to do this? Can get past feeling that the world is against you in order to make a stand for your own good? Dig deep within to find the ideas and the mental and spiritual resources to go beyond that which is limiting you, that which is giving you this feeling of poverty, or accept feeling impoverished. Maybe what you find is something you cannot change. You must now adapt our mind set to it. Create a paradigm in our mind in which this is acceptable. Appreciate the lessons that are presented with these circumstances and keep living life no matter what.

If the circumstances are unacceptable to you, work hard to change them, but don't whine. Don't complain. Don't act as though the world is against you, because it is not. This is just how life is right now. Put the effort in to change it, if changing it is what you most want.

Six of Creation

This is a simple truth- money is important. Money leads to happiness. Some people like to argue that. They will tell you that they don't need money to be happy, that they have all they need. Unless they have all the money they want, they are probably telling a lie.

With money you buy food. You buy clothes. You pay the bills associated with shelter- rent/mortgage, utilities, satellite TV, etc. When you have all you need without worry or fear over where it will come from, you can relax and are able to be happy. When you are not sure where it will come from, you are anxious, stressed and worried. Therefore, yes. Money does lead to happiness.

Consider money as energy. When you have what you need, that energy flows. When you don't, that energy becomes stuck. When the energy flow of financial needs gets stuck, sometimes it helps to receive a little stimulus to get it going again, or maybe a little something to help you until you get back on your feet again.

This act of helping those in need is not about the giver's ego, and neither is it about the receiver's. There is plenty of abundance in the world. All the money in the world is not intended for a single person. All the wealth to be had is not to be had by one entity. If you have all you need and more, then give when needed. You will still be provided for. You will still have enough for your desires and needs. It is common humanity to help the flow for another.

Seven of Creation

You know you are going to have a payback for your efforts, right? You know that the work you are putting in towards achieving your goals are not for nothing, don't you? It's all coming together. Is it taking longer

than you wanted? Too bad. Life is like that sometimes. This is not an invitation to give up. It's an invitation to keep doing what you are doing and have faith that it is all for an ultimate good.

Things are going to happen at their own pace and sometimes there is little you can do to make it go faster. The best you can do is have patience and not try to rush anything too much. You've worked hard, and that hard work is paying off. You never expected over night results, so why worry that things are not going faster? You knew when you started that it would take a while. Notice how far you have come? See how much your efforts have paid off already? Hang in there a little longer and you will have the results you set out to achieve. It really is that simple.

It's not like nothing has happened. It's not as if there has been no progress made. Look at how much you have accomplished already. It can be a good idea sometimes to reflect on the progress that you have made. Instead of fretting over what more there is to do, how about appreciating what you have achieved so far?

Eight of Creation

Y̲ou will find at times that a steady, focused routine will net the results that are appropriate to the situation. You don't always have to reinvent the system. No, what has always worked will continue to always work.

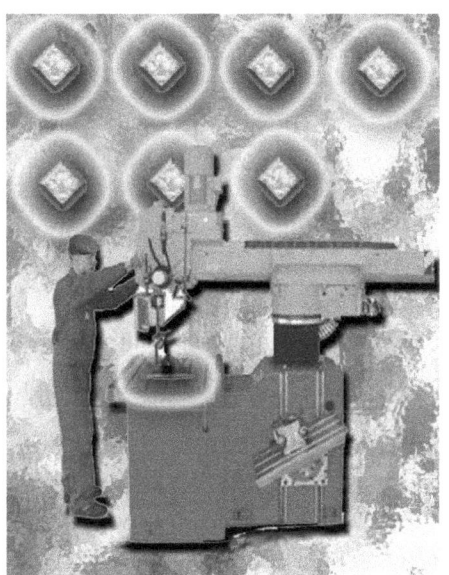

There are times when just doing your job is all that is needed of you. The best results may come from following a routine. Get focused, get in a groove, and just let the work flow.

Sometimes in life, that is exactly what a situation calls for. You do not always need to break new ground. You are not being called upon to make new discoveries or go above and beyond the call of duty. Sometimes all that is needed to see the best results is to do what is expected of you and nothing more.

Imagine a check out person at the grocery store. Consider their routine- scan the price of the items, put items in a bag, receive payment, make change if necessary, and send the customer on their way. Done. Would it be necessary for this person to reinvent the system with every customer? No, the way it has always been is just fine. Leave well enough alone.

You can even treat this as a Zen practice. As you follow the routine of your tasks, create an active meditation around it. Follow the flow of the work. Where does your mind drift? Where does the routine take your thoughts? The routine of the work may be boring, but your mind can make it anything you want it to be.

Nine of Creation

Independence. There is satisfaction in being able to do your own thing in your own way. It feels good to survey your accomplishments and know that what you have, you gained on your own. Where we put our attention,

what we are mindful of is what grows. When you work hard and put in the effort to achieve, then you can expect great results.

Consider that seed of prosperity that is the Ace of Creation. What did you do with it? Did you nurture it? Did you coax it to life? Did you provide the necessary elements for it to grow tall and strong with deep roots for a firm foundation? If so, now you can harvest the results. This is what dedication brings. It brings abundance.

Determination and willpower are crucial here. When you are focused, when you know the results you want to achieve and can see those results on the horizon, you must not be distracted by self-doubt. You must keep your sights on your goal and let nothing get you off track. If you do get off track, realign yourself with that horizon you are headed for and continue on, for it is your own determination that will get you there. Keep working at it until you have achieved your goals. There is tremendous satisfaction in doing your own thing and actually getting it done.

Ten of Creation

A strong family means that when problems arise, they are not simply dismissed. Solutions are sought and they are found. Problems are not swept under the carpet, and they are not met with denial. They are faced

head on and nobody backs down from them until they are solved. Insist on this, no matter what. Keep a group and a family strong. Each member is important and each member is entitled to feel valued.

You have the capacity to be the way-seer of a strong family or group unit. Tap into your strength and find the fortitude to provide the unwavering vision that keeps the family or the group a cohesive unit with each member applying their talents for the good of the individual, as well as the group. Stay solid in your commitment, and see to it that the weaknesses of the individual members are compensated for by the strengths of the others.

Generate prosperity. Be the provider. What does this family, this group need for its comfort and for its continued growth? How can you bring this? Use your intuition, your skills, your talents, and your willingness to try just about anything to provide.

Student of Creation

As a Student of Creation, you have confidence that things will always work out. Perhaps you have a sensation of lack. Maybe you don't feel like you have enough. But should you be worried? There is no reason to be!

Know that what you need will come to you. Know that financial security will manifest for you. Do you need to know exactly how? Be comfortable not knowing, just as the fool is comfortable taking a leap without knowing exactly how he will land.

What if the landing isn't smooth? What if you crash on the rocks below? You will mend swiftly and be undeterred as you continue down the path of life. You will be stronger and better for the experience. You will have learned the lessons that the experience was designed to teach you, and accept them as just that- lessons to be learned. Will you place blame and claim martyrdom? Absolutely not. You will appreciate the growing experience and use it as strength. You are always moving forward, never remaining stuck in what's behind you.

In terms of financial matters, take a chance. Sometimes these chances are calculated. You consider the implications and the options and are confident. Other times, you are not so calculated. Sometimes you gamble with your money and hope to win. Sometimes you jump into what you think is a great opportunity to get ahead with some investment or other. Maybe it works out for the best. Maybe it doesn't. What is important is, that when it doesn't you don't whine or complain. You learn what is meant to be learned and move on. All is well and remains that way.

You have no doubts. The universe knows what you need, and it's not going to let you go without. Your needs will be provided. You are learning, and are not afraid of the learning process. Sometimes the process of learning can include pain. So what? Get past the pain and before you know it, the lesson is integrated into who you are. Don't be afraid of the learning process. Learn what you can from every experience, and soon you will go beyond being a student and you will become a master.

Champion of Creation

Self-assured. Confidence. Faith in your own abilities. The ability to transcend limitations and blocks. Let these words describe you as the Champion of Creation. Tap into the power that these words represent. You have it in you. You have the ability to achieve, and you know this. Don't forget it.

When you think of Champions, do you imagine somebody who gives up? Somebody who says, "It's too difficult. I can't do it?" No. Champions inspire images of winners doing whatever it takes to accomplish their goals. They are the alpha dogs, the go-getters, the doers. You have that champion within you. Tap into that determined energy and let nothing stop you. Get it done. Do it. Be sure of yourself, and nothing can stop you. Things may slow you down, sure. That happens in life. But true power and strength is to get past them, get around, go over them, tunnel under them- whatever it takes to get on the other side of it and leave it behind you. Let confidence be your guiding light. You are a powerful being. Use your power!

There is no time for self-doubt. There is no room for negative thoughts degrading your self-image. You know what you are capable of. You know what you want to achieve, so do it. Why ruin a good thing with negativity? Silence the voices of doubt with measurable accomplishments. You are capable of such things. Do them boldly and without hesitation.

Mother of Creation

As the Mother of Creation, you are a sensitive being- sensitive to all beings. You have a love of all these beings, and feel this love returned to you. Not all of this love will come from humans. Much of this love comes from the four legged creatures of the earth. Much of it is given by the winged creatures in the air and in the trees. Much of this love comes from the rooted species of the earth- the trees, the plants, the flowers, the herbs, and the grass you walk on, the sand of the beach. There is a oneness to be shared with these beings, and just as you are nurtured by them, so too do you nurture them in return just by caring, and by your positive actions on their behalf.

Be like a mother who will do just about anything for her children. Nurture and provide. When one is in need, appreciate their cause. Just knowing you care enough to do so will in itself, make a tremendous difference. You have such a capacity to make a difference, and you don't even think about it. When something needs to be done, you simply do it. By doing it, the lives of others are enhanced. Your intuition is strong, your deeds are powerful, and the world is a better place because of it.

Father of Creation

As the Father of Creation you are shrewd in your business dealings and determined in your negotiations. You know the value of the dollar and are adept at drawing abundance and prosperity to yourself. You are

able to find and understand opportunities to generate wealth and income. You are a leader who is highly respected.

You are somebody who is simply good at what you do, and should somebody need your help, you will extend it to them. You will not, however, be expected to give handouts. You feel good about helping others, but are mindful of those who will take advantage of your generosity. Will you simply give money away? Or will you offer a loan? You take deserving people under your wing and generously teach what you know.

Likewise, you are a good and solid provider. In terms of relationships, you are somebody who takes good care of the people you care about, it is your pleasure to do so. You are a strong parental figure, a caring and giving partner, and a generous soul.

Speculation: *Mental Energy*
Ace of Speculation
SWORDS

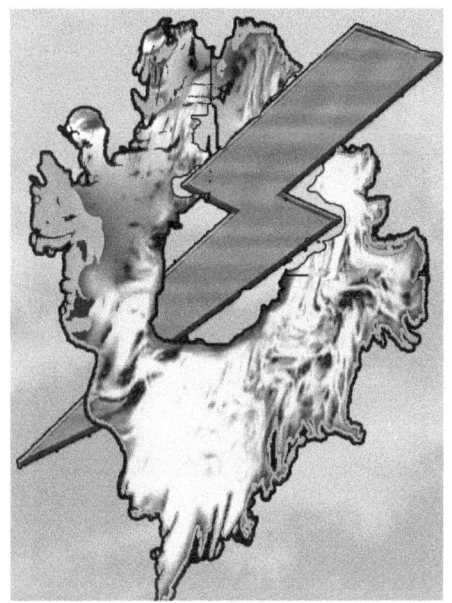

Quit doubting yourself. You were not put on this earth to be limited. You are here to express your brilliance, and yes, you have lots of it. If an idea occurs to you, if it pops into your head, if it is important to you, then it is worthy of exploration. Stop doubting. Stop making excuses. Stop believing that you are not good enough.

Sometimes an idea will come to you, seemingly from out of nowhere. Have you noticed this? You all of a sudden have an idea about something you weren't even thinking about? Have you ever wondered why this happens? It happens because thoughts are not ours to claim or to take credit for. Thoughts are there. They exist in the universal sub-consciousness. We simply become a vessel for them. When we become a vessel for a particularly powerful thought or idea, we are said to have "inspiration." When it comes to you, see where you can take it. What can you do with this great idea? Don't let it go to waste. If you don't do anything with it, it will simply be picked up by the next person. Why not be the one to do something great with it?

Powerful thoughts have a way of multiplying. For this reason, it is beneficial to surround yourself with positive people. Thoughts become our reality. By virtue of the fact that thoughts are contagious- that is to say they have a way of spreading from one person to another by the simple act of verbal and vibrational osmosis, is it not true that we take on the thoughts

149

and ideas of others as our own? So why tolerate negativity? Surround yourself with people who are thinking positive!

This is particularly true of weak and insecure people who seek validation by forcing their thoughts onto others with the intention of forcing an agreement. This is also true of weak and insecure people who are unsure and mistrusting of their ability to come up with a good idea of their own. They latch onto an idea of others without necessarily evaluating its validity and pertinence to their own situation. That said; trust your ability to channel positive thoughts. You really do have the power. Surround yourself with others who do the same. Together, the reality you create will be one well worth living in. Stay positive.

Two of Speculation

What does it mean to have a balanced mind? Do your thoughts balance one another, or is there a degree of conflict in what you are considering or thinking? Are you able to make up your mind and not be

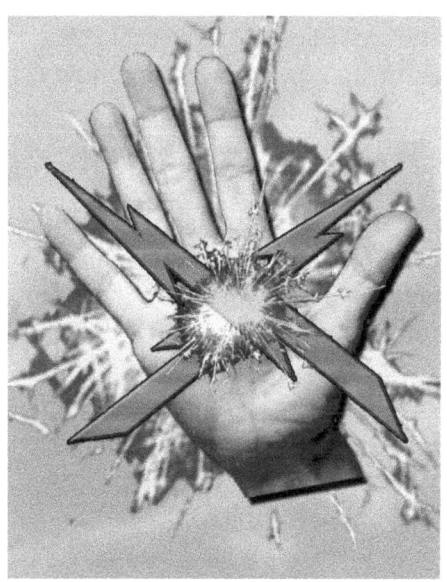

easily swayed from your decision? The ability to focus on a decision and come to a sound conclusion is a quality of a balanced mind.

The ability to see eye to eye with other people is an indication of balance in the mind. Hear what others have to say. Take their thoughts into consideration. Get your ideas out there too. Hear. Be heard. Create synergy. Don't be washed away in the thoughts and ideas of others, but do not be so hard-headed with your own ideas that you don't consider other's too. Together, your thoughts create a powerful force.

Where does your mind exist? Is it in a place of harmony, or are you looking for fights and for arguments? Do you appreciate what others have to say and their input in a situation, or does it have to be your way or no way? Are you open to equanimity?

Have a clear vision of what you want. When you are clear with our own thoughts, and are seeing eye to eye with another, positive actions can then occur. There will be harmony with these interactions and strength will result.

Three of Speculation

Our thoughts can be brutal. They can really take a toll on our body. We get stuck in negative thought patterns and ideas, and we forget that it is all in our mind. When we are in pain, we convince ourselves that what

we are experiencing is intrinsic to who we really are. We created this pain with our thoughts, and now they are torturing us. It happens.

Having expectations of people can stagnate you. Have you ever noticed this? You focus so much on one person and what you hope for from them, that they will only let you down. How can they not? It was you who placed all those hopes and dreams in this one entity. This often happens in terms of relationships. Ask yourself though, is their life solely focused on you? This is an unreasonable expectation, so don't expect it. As you are so focused on this person, you are denying yourself of the energy of others around you. How can this not lead to heartache, especially if this relationship is simply not meant to happen?

Don't focus too intently your energy on only one person. This person is probably not congruent with your highest and greatest good. Appreciate what there is to appreciate about them, but be mindful that any sense of disharmony or disappointment you may feel is coming from you. They are not projecting this onto you. This is your own reaction to an internal feeling of separation. This sense of separation comes from a hope and a desire you had concerning this other person that is in your mind that went unfulfilled. This is not the problem of the other person and should not be projected onto them. Allow them to live their life in accordance with their own highest good.

Break free of the stagnation by not holding tightly to a desired outcome from any one person. Break free of stagnation by appreciating and show-ing appreciation for a wide variety of people. Trust that what you need will come your way. Trust that by spreading your energy around, that it will connect with people who are in your best interest to connect with.

A great many people have energetic gifts for you. You will find them by not stagnating on one person. You will find them by spreading your energy and not focusing too intently on the one or ones who are clearly elsewhere emotionally, mentally and spiritually. That is to say, don't obsess over any one individual person. Don't give them the power over you to decide if you get to be happy or not. That is ridiculous.

We give people this power over us when we obsess over them, when we decide that we can only be happy, content and in harmony when they meet our conditions. You bring about your own unhappiness when you do this. For this person to live up to your expectations is an impossible demand. How can it not be? Accept and appreciate them, but don't expect too much. Expecting too much creates disharmony that ripples outward. You create disharmony for both yourself and the other person. Did this other person ask you to obsess over them? Do they want all this from you? Clinging too tightly to an expectation from them will only drive them crazy. Accept reality as it is and move on.

Four of Speculation

Take a rest. Turn your brain off and don't feel pressured to think too much. Thinking too much has a way of causing exhaustion, fatigue, worry, anxiety, fear, and a whole host of other unhealthy side effects. So

relax. Take it easy. Don't let your thoughts run your life. At least for a little while.

Perhaps you are worrying too much. Be advised to be rational about your fears and concerns. When you relax and do not react strongly to them, you will see your thoughts in a new light.

Meditate. Go beyond your thoughts and worries. Beyond them is a whole other plateau of understanding. Reach this other plateau and you will discover other truths about what it is that concerns you. You will likely find that they are attached to nothing that can't be dealt with. You will find these answers when you are relaxed and not desperately searching.

Five of Speculation

It doesn't matter who won or who lost. That's not what the issue is here. What matters is that it is over. It is time to breathe a sigh of relief, regroup, pick up the pieces, rebuild, and get on with life. What was this argument about, anyway? What started the fight? It's over. Put it behind you.

None of us are alone on the planet. We all must share space with others. That is just a simple truth.

Here's what happens- you have ideas. You often project these ideas onto others. You have attitudes. You project these attitudes onto others. You generate thought forms that others must live with. Not everybody will like what you are projecting. You will not like everything others project either. There may come a breaking point where somebody, maybe yourself, cannot take it anymore and something erupts- an altercation, an argument, or maybe a slew of harsh words.

You emit energy that others are picking up on. Some of us are highly sensitive to these things, and we feel them so much stronger than others. As you are doing these things, whether you do it consciously or not, others are doing the same.

We are constantly living in the energetic soup that we co-create simply by being alive. Sometimes what we project is harmonious and congruent with the will of others, sometimes it is not. When it is not, conflicts may very well be the result.

Sometimes living with the energy of others can be a bit much. Sometimes for the sake of your own sanity, you must put yourself first. This is not a greedy or selfish thing to do. This is basic human survival. As much as you are there for others, sometimes you just need to focus on yourself. Do what you can to escape the energy bubbles created by others, and be in your own space. You will thank yourself for this one small gift. By accepting this, you may avoid unnecessary conflicts and promote peace and harmony for yourself and for others as well.

Six of Speculation

Guess what? Every one of us goes through this. We have a hard time. Life gets turbulent, and we need help from others. There is not a human on the planet that has not been through this at one time or another. It is not a weakness to admit to needing help. A weakness is to need help

but deny it. Strength is to admit to needing help and surrendering to the powers that can provide it. Set your sights on a distant shore and say, "Over there, I will heal." And then allow ourselves to be taken there.

"Getting help" can take on a number of forms. It can be professional help. Can a psychiatrist help you? Then go to a psychiatrist. Can an Alcoholics Anonymous meeting help you? Then go to an Alcoholics Anonymous meeting. Will checking into a rehab clinic help you? Then check into a rehab clinic. Will talking to a good friend just to hear their voice help you? Then talk to a good friend just to hear their voice. Will listening to your favorite song relax you and help you feel better? Then listen to your favorite song.

Whatever help you need, get it. Simple as that. Keep this one intrinsic fact in mind- happiness is your birthright. If there is something keeping you from living the fullest, greatest, happiest life possible, investigate why. If you can't figure it out, enlist the proper people to help you. If you do know, but you realize you can't fix it on your own, get the help you need to fix it. There is never a point to being miserable, so don't accept that as the norm of your life.

Seven of Speculation

Sometimes you simply don't want to open your heart. Sometimes you'd rather keep to yourself and not feel the pressure to be at one with others. Maybe you don't want people knowing your business. Maybe you don't want others fussing over you. Maybe you would rather not have to fuss over anybody else. Perhaps you want to keep yourself to yourself for yourself. Maybe there is something on your mind and you'd prefer a little personal space over a hug from somebody.

Sometimes, just be aloof. Go ahead. You're allowed to be. How crucial is it that everybody knows everything about you? Maintain some mystery. What is nobody's business but your own, keep to yourself. Let people wonder about you. What's wrong with that? Nothing. Get your heart off of your sleeve. Keep things to yourself. Share what you want to share when you want to share, but don't let anybody make you feel obligated to, because you are not. Be you in any way you feel like being yourself. As long as you do so within the bounds of the laws and rules of society, you don't have to explain yourself. Let others adjust. Let others adapt. Let others figure you out

Be a quiet force. Make your plans in private. Surprise people with what you have been planning. Work. Achieve. Share. When you are ready, when everything is in place, then let people see the brilliance of your true self. Don't give too much away too soon. Don't let people in on the inner workings of your great masterpiece. Accomplish great things quietly and let them ask, "How did you do that?" Be amazing this way. Be mysterious. Mystery equals intrigue. Intrigue equals advantage. Create advantages for yourself by keeping quiet. Can you do it? Some can. Some can't. Practice at it.

Eight of Speculation

You create our own reality with the thoughts you think and how you interpret your environment and your situations. If you see things as a negative, that is what your life becomes. If you interpret what seems to be a negative situation as an opportunity to learn and to grow, then that is what it becomes. It becomes a classroom creating growth opportunities.

Your mind can create ropes that bind you and keep you from moving forward. These ropes are the idea that you are stuck, that you can't or should not move forward. This is a very limited view. You are stuck in a mindset, that is all. You are not, in any actuality, truly bound by anything, no matter how real it seems.

It is as if you feel the ropes and your mind immediately goes to the idea of ropes and constriction. Constriction equals oppression. Oppression equals impossible situation. What you need to do is open your eyes, take off the blindfold and see reality as it is, that what you believes is an impossible situation is only impossible because you are telling yourself it is. Intrinsically speaking, however, there is nothing earthly or spiritually keeping you in bondage to any situation. You can leave anytime. Change you attitude and the ropes simply fall away. Now you are free.

Nine of Speculation

The brain, when used properly is a wonderful tool. One of the original uses for our brain, our mind, our thoughts, was to put into action what our emotions, reflexes, and intuition were telling us. Originally,

intuition and spirit were accepted as the true wisdom of a human being. The brain's job was to take into consideration what it was that spirit had to say, and what it needed, and then create and implement a plan in accordance with this. At some point in human advancement however, the brain got the idea it knew what was best for the spirit, and staged a coup.

The ego evolved and soon intuition and spirit were all but ignored in an average human being. Where intuition and spirit once held dominion over the self, they became relegated to a small squeaky voice screaming to be heard.

With the mind screaming so loudly, certain problems arise. You reap what you sew. It's been said so many times in so many contexts, but it is still a good concept to consider when looking at the effects your mind has on you. Where has your mind been? Has it been fixated on all that is wrong, all that cannot be fixed, and all that is terrible and unharmonious in life? Well guess what will happen? These thoughts are going to add up to a plethora of grief which will manifest in a number of ways. You may experience them as sadness, nervousness, anxiety, worry, tension, illness.

161

The solution is to let go of the need to control and then simply go with the flow. Trust spirit. Trust intuition. Instead of forcing your thoughts in a direction they are not organically meant to go, accept the true direction they are meant to go and surrender to the flow. Once you are with the flow of your spirit, life gets so much easier. You are less prone to both dis-ease and disease. You're not going to be beating yourself up, and you are not going to hide your face from the world, seeing it through the filter your tears are creating.

Consider what thoughts you are holding onto that do not serve the needs of your spirit. Do you know intuitively that things are going to work out one way, but insist on forcing it in another direction? Would it be best to accept the paradigm that is real, and readjust your thoughts around it accordingly? Consider carefully and honestly what thoughts represent your highest and best truth, and which are mere fabrications. If they are mere fabrications, let them go. They serve only to cause stress and grief. Take inventory and clean the clutter of your mental house.

Ten of Speculation

We all go through this. We get so caught up in worry and frustration and fear and all such matters of negative thought that we finally can't take it anymore. Are any of us immune to this? Do we not all experience worry and fear? It is a natural human thing to do. Sometimes, it becomes so overwhelming that we simply have a breakdown. We have reached a point where we simply cannot take it anymore. We hit the bottom. The good news is though, that once there, now we can heal and bounce back up.

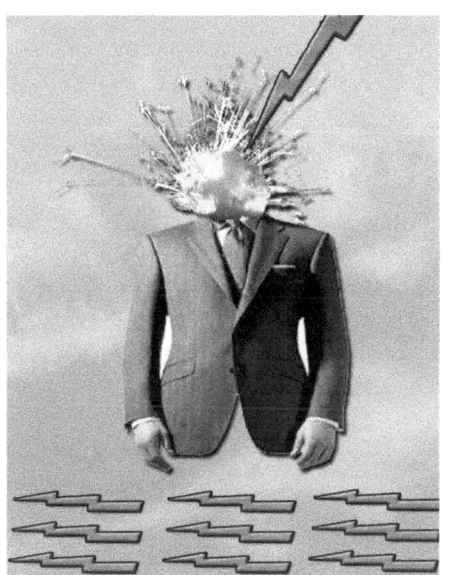

The trick to not letting your thoughts do this to you is to identify negative thoughts as you experience them, without letting them take root. By taking root, they will sink into your soul and drain you of energy. But that does not mean deny them. Acknowledge your feelings and realize that they have a message for you. Observe them, take the message you need from them, and then let them drift away.

That is the goal- to release the negativity that may be sinking in. Be mindful too, that what you may be feeling may not even be originating with you. How sensitive are you to other people's energy? Some of us are highly sensitive to the vibes others are putting out. You may be feeling their negativity, if you can't identify it within yourself. Do what you can to shield yourself from this. It is not meant for you to be effected by the energy of other people.

Take stock of what you are feeling. Analyze any negative feelings you may be having and see if you can trace them to where they are coming from. What can you do to experience these feelings fully and be released of them? By experiencing them fully, you become their master, and they, not the master of you. Experience them, and then let them go. Holding onto them will only allow them to sink deeper and deeper into your being. Let them go. Be free. Be light. Bounce back.

Student of Speculation

As the Student 0f Speculation, you may say "I'm not sure what's going to happen, but I'm going to try. Wish me luck." You have a true curiosity that needs to be explored. You are not merely content to read

an answer in a book. No. You are somebody who needs to experience for yourself what the answer is.

In the process of satisfying your curiosity, you may get into situations that others consider unwise or dangerous, but you trust that the answer is worth the risk taken to find it. Sometimes incredible discoveries are this way, such as "Yes, electricity can be harnessed for use by man." Other times, discoveries such as attaching jet engines to a car will kill you if you try to drive it. Come what may, it takes a Student of Speculation to ask the questions that lead to these discoveries.

You have an insatiable wanting to learn more and more. You are asking questions and seeking answers. You are studying. You are researching. You will pursue your interests with enthusiasm, but you may not stick with it. You may change interests quickly and want to try new things frequently. Sometimes you simply do not have the drive to stick with it to follow through to the final answer. You may get bored with it and move on to something else quickly. Your brain may be so active, that such focus is difficult.

165

Champion of Speculation

As the Champion of Speculation, you are determined. But are you mindful of others? Do you notice anybody you may be overrunning? Are you giving thought to others who might be in your path? You may

seem very abrasive, self-centered, and cold. Perhaps this may be true, but the reality is you very focused on the task at hand. You have a strong idea of what you want to achieve, and you let nothing stop you in your pursuits. In a perfect sense, this can be a positive thing. You are very goal oriented.

Unfortunately though, this "take no prisoners" attitude is not always the best approach. Sometimes, you do have to be mindful of others. Others may have ideas about a situation and will want to be heard. Your personality is stubborn and opinionated, unlikely to consider other viewpoints. Things have to be your way, and that's all there is to it. This personality can be difficult to tolerate.

However, you are also likely to be a loyal friend. You are somebody who will go to bat for anybody you believe in. You are likely to stand up for them and even fight for these people, standing by them unwaveringly.

Your determination and drive to succeed makes you a natural leader. Somebody has to have the drive. Somebody has to have the vision. Somebody has to have the determination to achieve perfection. You have the ability to delegate tasks and make sure everybody does their part.

Mother of Speculation

As the Mother of Speculation, you are not afraid to speak your mind. This is both your greatest power and your greatest weakness. It is your power in that when something needs to be said, when something needs to be communicated no matter how blunt, painful, or simply hard to say it is, you are able to say it with conviction and authority.

Maybe the truth will make you unpopular. Perhaps what needs saying will be met with resistance by those who are not ready or willing to hear it. Be that as it may, it still needs saying, so somebody needs to say it.

It is your weakness in that sometimes you do not consider carefully the best way to say what needs saying. "Bedside manners" as we say of doctors. Perhaps you may not be as delicate or soft with your words as those for whom you have a message may like you to be. Whatever the case, you are adept at saying what needs to be said.

You may come across as cold, maybe even heartless, but this is probably not the truth of who you are. You are not as concerned with appearances as others may be. You are not trying to be liked or win any popularity contests. You are concerned with getting to the heart of whatever the matter may be.

There are times when this is a tremendous gift, especially when dealing with a difficult circumstance. When things are tough, somebody has to

167

come forward and be a spokesperson. This person, becoming the public figure for the situation will have to bear the brunt of the criticism from the masses for it. You can take it. You have what it takes to toughen up and be thick skinned enough to not take criticism personally.

Sometimes though, you must adapt. You must employ empathy and become what people need you to be. Not every situation calls for toughness. Sometimes it is necessary to feel what the others are feeling and present the truth to them in a way that they are easily able to receive it. This can be challenging for the you, but those who are able to master it, often live the best of both worlds- both the world of absolute truth, and the world of compassion and empathy for others.

Father of Speculation

As the Father of Speculation, you always seem to have the answer. You are not just making stuff up to sound intelligent. You actually do know what you are talking about. If you don't have an answer, you can point somebody in the right direction to find it. You are very skillful with words. You are right at home speaking and seldom fumble for the right thing to say. "Uhm" and "uh…" simply are not a part of your vocabulary.

You are a master of logical and clear thought and can be very persuasive. You are a natural leader and a quick problem solver. You don't settle for less. Perfection is important to you. You get right to the heart of the matter and do not let the petty and mundane drag you down. You are quick to grasp complicated concepts and can easily make the difficult understandable.

You will be the one to examine a situation and question it. You will find what is at the root of any confusion by way of a clear and analytical mind. It can be daunting, but you are up to the challenge. As Rudyard Kipling wrote, "If you can keep your head when all about you are losing theirs…"

This is something that can happen- Everybody is reacting without examining what it is they are reacting to, and nobody seems to be thinking straight. This has the effect of generating chaos. It becomes an epidemic as everybody takes the cues from the others, reacting as they are without anybody actually knowing what it is that they are freaking out over. That's where your power comes into play. You will cut through the mental fog and become the beacon of clear thought. You are a master of logic and clarity.

You are the one with the answers, and others know this. They will flock to you with questions. Do your best to answer sincerely. If you don't know the answers though, simply say "I don't know." You don't have to pretend to know something you don't to impress others. You will be more impressive by admitting your limits.

Your ideas will be sought after. You have time and time again proven yourself to be a brilliant person. It is just expected of you now. Appreciate this. Help others to figure out what they need to figure out.

Desire: *Emotional Energy*
Ace of Desire
CUPS

Consider these words from Sri Bhagavan, the avatar of Oneness: "Life is to be experienced; anything when experienced completely is bliss." Apply this wisdom to your emotions.

Of course, it is easy to appreciate your emotions when they are positive. But the reality of your existence is that you are here to experience a much greater range of feelings than just this. There is also what we usually categorize as negative. You will feel sad. You will feel anger, remorse, heartbreak and disappointment. What do you do with these feelings? Often, it is your natural inclination to suppress them. You push them down. You deny them. These are unpleasant to you, so you hide them and pretend that they are not there. But does this mean they go away?

Denying your emotions does not eliminate them. It only puts them on hold until later. These feelings will pop up again, and when they do, they will be just as potent as ever. How many suppressed emotions does an average person carry about with them? How much have we all pushed down, tried to forget and tried to abandon? Within most all of us there is an uncountable number of such feelings. These have accumulated since before our ability to remember.

Follow the advice from Sri Ammabhagavan. Whatever it is you are feeling, no matter how uncomfortable or miserable it makes you, stay with it. Experience it. Feel it completely and examine what it has to teach you. Ride it

171

out. Don't suppress it, don't medicate it, and don't deny it. When it has run its course, it will be gone. When it is gone, in its place will be bliss. This is true. This works.

Cry, grieve, shout, scream, laugh, sing, dance, do whatever you must to experience your feelings fully. Just don't give up on yourself or your ability to cope. Whatever negativity you may experience, it will pass. When it does pass, expect a sense of "Finally. It's about time." Now joy has arrived. Now you experience bliss. Now you can breathe a sigh of relief and be glad.

Of course though, the same can be said of positive emotions- joy, happiness, love, gratefulness, appreciation, to name a few. Hold onto these and experience them as completely as you can. These elevate your vibration. These simply make you feel good. Experience these to their fullest potential and enjoy every minute of them.

Two of Desire

Consider cups as vessels for your desires and the condition your heart is in. An upright cup is capable of holding love. An overturned or broken cup has been damaged. Overturned cups tell us that something has not gone right. Your desires are not contained. They are leaking out. There is sadness and disappointment in the air.

Visualize two upright cups. One is in your hand. The other is in the hand of somebody you care deeply about. See the two of you exchanging cups. Smile while you do it. Feel good. Feel great. Feel absolute bliss. Would you offer your cup, your heart, to somebody that you did not absolutely trust with it?

Do not be afraid that the other will take your heart lightly. Know instinctively that your heart is in good hands with this other person. At the same time, they are aware of the trust placed in them. They will not betray the sensitivity and the vulnerability of your heart. They will take care with your heart. Let there be trust, harmony, and love.

This is an earthly kind of love. This is part of what life on earth is meant to be, so enjoy the harmony, love, and friendship of the people you are the closest to. It is part of what life on earth is meant to be. We all incarnated on the earth for a reason, and one of those reasons was to generate such friendships and relationships. Enjoy them. See where they go. They are a big part of what makes life good.

Three of Desire

Celebrate. Have ceremonies. Appreciate a sense of community and friendship where the good fortune of one is a cause for joy in all. What do you have to celebrate? Let others in on it. Let it become a shared

victory. Your glories are all the sweeter for the fellowship they inspire.

What about your friends? What about your family? What is happening in their life that is cause for good cheer? Don't hold back on your praise. Don't hold back on your congratulations. Let them know and truly feel that you are a part of their life by boosting their glory with some heart-felt well wishes.

Be mindful, you are a part of a much bigger whole. You are but an aspect of the greater community around you. Share the joys of this community. Also, be a part of the healing. We all get wounded. We all need to heal. Help others to do so without judgment. Reach out, and at the same time, be reachable. Appreciate others, and be appreciated. Be an active member in your community. You truly will make a difference this way.

Four of Desire

Do you ever sit around with your arms folded and a pouty look on your face? Can people all but hear you say, "Hmmph" in defiance of a situation? Do you act like a child who did not get their own way? Like

one who was told he can't play video games until he finishes his homework? But he doesn't want to do his homework, so he just sits there brooding, daring anybody to tell him what to do. Eventually, of course, this will pass. Before long, he will get over what is bothering him and he will feel better. But for now, he is going to sit in his own negativity no matter how irrational it may seem to others.

When you get this way, get over it. Whatever is bothering you, examine it fully until you realize that it really doesn't matter. What you are obsessing over is, in all actuality, inconsequential. The sooner you get past it, get over it, the sooner you will re-energize yourself and accomplish much better things than throwing a tantrum.

Or maybe you are simply bored. Sometimes, you get so stuck in the idea that you don't know what you should do. So what do you do? You do nothing. Rather than find the energy to do something, you just sit and ponder all the things you should be doing. Do you do them, or do you just sit and ponder them? It's a rather silly endeavor, but it is something each of us does from time to time. This is another way to define procrastination. If you know you need to do something, get up and do it! Thinking about it is not the same as doing it, so quit thinking, and do!

Ask yourself, "What should I be doing?" The answer will come to you. When the answer does come, do not second guess it. Get up and do it. Listen to the answer that just came to you, and act on it.

Get over whatever is bothering you and embrace a more positive attitude. Why let things bother you? This only keeps you stuck in the mud of despair. Get past it and you will prosper. This is guaranteed.

Five of Desire

Imagine walking through a field littered with overturned cups. The sky is bleak with darkness and low hanging, heavy clouds. Keep in mind cups symbolize your heart, what you carry your emotions in. When the cup is

upright and steady, your emotions are balanced. You are happy. You feel loved, and you have a sense of well-being.

But what of these overturned cups? Here, the love and the glad feelings have spilled out. This is disappointment and a sense of loss. Look around one more time. Do you see that not every cup is overturned? Not all is lost here. There is still hope. The sky won't stay dark forever. Whatever rain is going to fall from those clouds will do so and the sky will be blue again. The sun will shine, and you will get over what is bothering you.

Sadness and disappointment never linger endlessly. They are contingent upon a situation in which you have an expectation, or a hope that does not go your way. Once you adjust your thinking to be congruent with the paradigm that exists, you experience joy again. The sky turns from a bleak gray to a bright blue. Your mood shifts. The sun comes out and you feel better.

Six of Desire

How can the memories of yesterday empower you today? Think back to a particularly warm memory, one that makes you feel good inside. Take a moment to bask in this nostalgia. Relive it in your mind the best

you can. Try to experience again the aromas of the memory, the sensory experiences of touch, sight, and sound. What did you hear during this memory? What did you feel? See? Smell? What feelings did you experience in the occurrence of this instance? Conjure these as best you can. Take it into your heart as though it were happening right here and right now. There is power here. Bring this empowerment into your world today.

Of course, the past is in the past. Life is lived in the now. But remember, yesterday's "now" doesn't simply vanish because it gave way to the next now… the next now… and the next now. These "nows" of yesterday become part of your DNA. They are a part of your subconscious. They will return to you in unexpected moments, dreams, and a simple desire to re-feel the feelings you had. So how can you relive these "nows" long gone?

You can relive them by appreciating what you have in your life today, this "now." You can relive them by giving your full attention to the people who you share your time and your life with today. They may or may not be the same people as yesterday, but that shouldn't matter. Show them love. Show them appreciation. Let them know you are glad that they are in your life now. When you do this, you are creating new memories to look back fond-ly on during a "now" to come.

Remember a truly great moment and bring it to your present. Relive it. Do you have photographs to look at that will remind you of it? Do you have a song that will take you back to that time? Is there a certain food that will place you solidly in that time? How about an old favorite movie you have not watched in some time? Is there an old friend you can reconnect with? Honor too, those people, pets, and things in your life right now that make life enjoyable. They are creating the warm memories you will have tomor-row.

Seven of Desire

Maintain a healthy and alive imagination. This can be very healing. There are many answers to the universe that can be found when you step away from rational and logical thought. Stepping away from rationality can reveal secret and hidden aspects of the universe, yourself, or a situation that you do not otherwise see.

Be a dreamer. Stick your heads in the clouds. Live in a fantasy world. Explore the world of "Could Be." In the World of Could Be, you will see the real true contents of your heart. Without the restrictions of "what really is" you can figure out what it is you really want. Once you figure out what you really want, you begin the task of manifestation. So go beyond any and all limiting thoughts. Go crazy with what your real true desires are. There are no boundaries and there are no limitations. Put your head in the clouds and explore your heart's desire.

While doing this, though, it is important to keep your feet on the ground. Stay rooted. Stay grounded. It is easy to get lost in our own thoughts and imagination and feel like you've drifted away. There is divinity in the imagination. However, you are a being of the earth. This is why you must stay grounded. Why do you think we have gravity? Why do you think we are in human form? To utilize what we find in the imagination, we must be planted firmly on the earth. Be as a tree with deep roots that grows tall. Have a firm foundation with high and lofty ideals.

Having your head in the clouds, sometimes, can be the best place for it. Dream. Fantasize. Imagine. Visualize the most ideal situation for yourself. We all need to do this. Sometimes though, you really do need to come down to earth and pay attention to the practical matters of your life. Plant your feet on the ground and root in. Strong roots make for a strong foundation. The stronger your roots, the higher you are able to hold your head. Find balance between the world of fantasy and the practical matters of earthly life. This is to appreciate what both worlds have to offer in equal measure. Gaining this balance allows for the blending and sharing of the best of both worlds.

Eight of Desire

Sometimes, something in your life simply serves its purpose and then it is over. It can be sad to face. This might be something really great that brought you much happiness. But this happiness fades. You examine it

and you realize, it just isn't what it used to be. Then you come to the determination that it is time to bid it farewell. It is time to put it behind you and walk away.

Perhaps it is a relationship, perhaps it is a job, or perhaps it is a living situation. It could be just about anything. Things have a way of running their course in our life and then they are over. To try and cling to everything that comes our way only leads to spiritual and mental clutter. We can drive ourselves crazy that way. When it is time to let go, then do it. Let go.

There is no guilt involved here. You need not feel you are letting yourself, another person, or an entity down by walking away. There is no need to burn your bridges, and there is no need to attach anger or bitterness to it. When it is time, it is time, and you will know it. This is part of your growing process that you should not deny yourself. By staying when you should be going, you only stunt your growth. Be mindful of this, and don't do it.

Nine of Desire

Do you have a care in the world? If so, put them on the back-burner for the time being. Appreciate all the good things you have in your life. Take a moment to count your blessings and you will find them to be many.

The cups that hold your emotions are all perfectly upright. They are all perfectly aligned. They are polished and clean and do not have a single scratch or crack in them. There is no sadness here, no depression. This is complete satisfaction and appreciation. And why shouldn't there be? Life, after all, is good!

With life being this good, when you are feeling this great, what can't you accomplish? Take this joyous feeling and apply it to all aspects of your life. Remember the Law of Attraction- "That which is like unto itself is drawn." This positive energy will attract more and more positive energy. You will experience miracles as all you wish for is drawn to you. It's all in the attitude. Stay positive!

Ten of Desire

Take a look at your cups. Are any fallen over? Are any cracked? No. They are all standing upright. Not only are they standing upright, but they appear in a rainbow in the sky. There is a celebration. This is an

appreciation of life, of love, of happiness and complete contentment. There is joy. Children are dancing and having fun. This is a family at peace. The sky is blue and there is not a hint of any danger anywhere.

What though, was the journey to this perfect day? Did it happen all at once, or is this the destination after a long journey? Meditate on this. Imagine yourself as having arrived at destination after a long, difficult, often troublesome, sometimes delightful, sometimes wearisome, sometimes joyous, often miserable, many times happy journey.

Throughout this journey you have had this idea of the perfection you have been working towards. This has been an emotional journey. This has been a journey to open your heart and to fill it with things that matter to you. This has been a journey to discover for yourself what it is that love really means to you. Ask yourself, "What does love mean to me?"

What do you need out of the giving process? What do you expect in terms of receiving love? How well have you created and maintained a balance of these? Reflect on the joys of your life and recognize how far you have come. Appreciate the sense of completion. Appreciate the pain that taught you the lessons that have helped you understand who you are, what you need, and what your capacity to give is. Take stock of who is in your life and what they mean to you. Appreciate those you have found in earthy form with whom you share a spiritual and soul level bond.

Visualize a rainbow of cups in the sky. What fills each one of these cups? With whom do you share the bounty of these cups? Reflect on what is good in your life, and the people you share it with.

Student of Desire

As the Student of Desire, you are a sensitive person who feels feelings much deeper and more intense than most people. As such, you are prone to great bursts of joy, as well as deep and dark sadness. You are

likely sensitive to the energies of others, picking up on what they are feeling whether you realize you are doing so or not. As such you may often feel moody and not know why. As you feel the feelings of others, you may react to these feelings, confused as to why you feel this way. You may often be misunderstood by others who are unaware of your empathic nature.

Being sensitive this way, likewise, has the benefit of intuition when you are aware of this ability. Once you realize that you are sensitive to the energies of others, you can then master it. Instead of letting the energies of others overwhelm you, you can use them as a learning tool, not just about the people you are sensitive to, but to the very nature of the human race.

Your heart is very open as somebody who does not look for things to be wrong in a relationship or a situation. You are focused on what is good and wonderful. It could be that you are seeing the world through rose colored glasses, but at the same time, your optimism for what can be great can and should be contagious.

Champion of Desire

As the Champion of Desire, you have a perfect ideal of how you would like things to be, particularly when it comes to emotions. You like to idealize, and you like to project these ideals onto others. If these ideals of yours don't happen to fit what these other people feel in their own hearts, you may take it personally. As you take it personally, you may become upset. Because of this, you may be seen as moody. When what you project hits its mark though, and these other people appreciate what you are sending out, you shine. This truly puts you in your element.

You are most definitely a people person. You love to engage and be active with other people. At a party, chances are you are the center of attention. Likely, you have many friends. People are naturally drawn to you for your exuberant personality. But be careful. You run the risk of being overbearing. Not everybody will share your enthusiasm for togetherness. You run the risk of coming on to too strong, causing people to take a step back, lest they become overwhelmed.

Ideas suddenly pop into your head. You love to have fun, and to bring people into your circle to have fun together with. Your natural tendency to see the good in a situation makes you an optimistic and positive person. Sometimes, you may be a little too positive. A little too optimistic. You may sometimes deny the problems that exist, which does not do you any good.

Be realistic. It's great that you don't dwell in the negative, but accept things for what they are. When you always wear rose colored glasses and smile when you your heart is frowning you run the risk of coming across as phony. People will see through this mask. Be careful about that. Stay positive, but at the same time, stay real.

Project too much falseness, and people will stop taking you seriously. Nobody will care what you have to say because they will just assume that you are not being genuine. Don't end up dismissed every time you open your mouth because people know exactly what you are going to say. You're denying yourself important life lessons when you do this. Find the balance between reality and optimism.

Mother of Desire

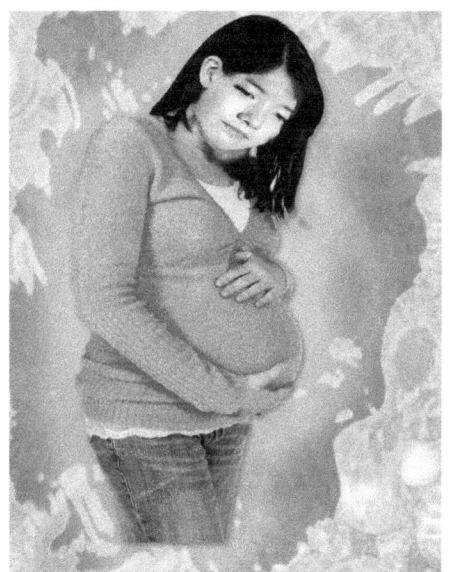

As the Mother of Desire, you care. You cannot stand to see any being in pain. When you know somebody, or some creature is hurting, you hurt right along with them. Because of this, you have a natural tendency towards healing. You want the best for others, just as any mother would for their child. To you, all the creatures, no matter how many legs, no matter if they have dominion of the land, skies, or sea, are your children. Your capacity to love and to express this love is great.

You are sensitive to the feelings of others. Your intuition is very in tune with the vibes that others are sending out. You may seem almost magical for your ability to know what somebody is thinking and what they are feeling,. This is often what you respond to. Somebody may say one thing, but in their heart, they mean something very different. You are not fooled by this. It is their heart that you respond to. This may amaze or sometimes confuse people, but it is a natural gift that you have. It is difficult for others to lie to you. You see the truth.

Your heart is your guide. You listen to it above and beyond all things. As a person who wants the best for all beings, you are likely to follow the instincts that provide this. It may or not be logical. You do your best to balance logic and intuition to create the best situation for those around you. You may at times sacrifice your own needs for those of others. This is just who you are. You appreciate it when people take notice of this and express gratitude, but you are not ruled by this need. The wellbeing of those you care about is reward enough.

Father of Desire

As the Father of Desire you are a compassionate person. You have walked many miles in many shoes. You have experienced fully the full range of human emotions and have endured the lows of life and celebrated the highs. You have seen much, done much, and experienced much. These experiences have not been passive happenings to be forgotten. No, each has been a learning and a growth opportunity. You have absorbed the experiences of life and have transformed it into empathy for others.

Your life experiences have added up to quite an illustrative patchwork of emotions, ambitions, knowings, and understandings. You have experienced just about every emotion there is to experience in human form, and now you are wise. As such, you have a vantage point from which to observe and appreciate the shoes others are walking in. From this vantage point you are qualified to offer advice, solace, compassion and understanding. You are generous with all these things, being both a friend and a rock. As an empath, identifying and recognizing the truth of another person beyond the shields and the masks they wear, you are well suited in the role of healer.

To be a true healer, one must have experienced pain. How can you appreciate and have empathy for the pain and suffering of another if you yourself cannot relate to it? This is one of your assets. You have experienced pain, suffering and heartbreak but you did not drown in these experienc-

191

es. No, you came out of it wiser, even thankful for the strength developed from it. You are willing and wanting to share this strength with all who need it.

In Conclusion...

Wondering how all this applies to you? Are you unsure of where you are on this journey to an Enlightened Life? Keep a few things in mind. Awakening and Enlightenment happens in increments. You have life experiences, and you learn from them. You have more life experiences and you learn from them too. As you learn, your awareness and consciousness expands. As this growth and expansion happens, you are open to more and more possibilities of knowings, knowledge, and wisdom.

Grand Enlightenment doesn't happen in a single lifetime. It takes uncountable incarnations to master all that needs to be mastered, so why rush it? How can your mind even possibly know where exactly you are on a journey that defies time?

All you can do is live the best life you can live this lifetime. Follow your inspirations and your intuition, and trust that they are taking you in the right direction. Listen to the voices that speak to you, and pay attention. Trust that everything and everybody in your life has a purpose, and honor their purpose by honoring them. Stay positive, and stay real. Keep your eye on your Star and follow it to your Personal Enlightenment. It's doable and it is reachable.

Asking the Cards

Of course, you can ask the Tarot Cards where you are on your journey. Separate the cards into Major Arcana and Minor Arcana piles. Ask the Major Arcana cards "What aspect of my spiritual self should I work on perfecting at this time?" Then pick one. Now meditate on it. What actions can you put into place to perfect this aspect of who you are?

Now ask, "What aspect of my spiritual self is the strongest?" Now pick another card. Do you agree with it? Why? Why not? Meditate now on that answer.

Ask now, "What is my greatest ambition to achieve this lifetime?" Pick a card. Does it surprise you? Scare you? Delight you? Thrill you? Disgust you? Confuse you? Captivate you? Inspire you?

Now turn your attention to the Minor Arcana Cards. Ask the cards, "What piece of myself can use some strengthening?" Now draw a card. Does it resonate with you? Can you understand why this card would come up for you? Use it as a focus for your mediation and work to understand and strengthen this aspect of yourself.

Ask now, "What is my strongest and best quality?" Pick a card. Any surprises here? If yes, why? If no, why not?

With or without the cards, focus on how you feel about the life you are living. What do you feel you are doing "right?" What do you feel you could be doing "better?" What are your proudest moments? What are your regrets? What moment in your life would you most like to relive? Redo? Re-examine? What can these moments tell you about who you are right now? Asking yourself these questions and looking honestly within for the answer can only give strength to your spirit.

The path of your life runs parallel and crisscross with so many others. We meet each other, greet each other, help each other, get in each other's way, love each other, dislike each other, tolerate each other. This is true. Just do what your intuition tells you is right, and no matter how you effect the life and the journey of others, trust you are doing the right thing. It may not seem like the right thing sometimes. You may have regrets and wonder if you did the right thing, but keep this in mind- in your actions a life lesson may have just been learned for this other person. A life lesson may have been learned for you in yours. Life is about the lessons we learn. As such, we are often the facilitators of these lessons for each other.

By being the best person you can be this lifetime, whatever "best" means to you, keeps you moving in the right direction down the path of life. It means to follow your instincts, your intuition and do what you know to be right for you.

You! Do what is best for your journey! Not somebody else's journey. Their journey is their journey. Your journey is your journey and that is what you are responsible for. Remember that. If you do this, you are on the path- the right path. You are living an Enlightened Life, and as such you are an inspiration for others. Keep going.

About Jim Larsen

Jim Larsen heard the call of tarot in 2004, and he listened. In so doing, his life changed completely. The call of tarot took Jim to the Big Island of Hawaii from his home and Virginia, and from there he has traveled the world, exploring and looking within for wisdom. Jim enjoys meditation, teaching English as a foreign language, writing, performing, Reiki, Deeksha, hiking, and basking in the sun.

Also by Jim Larsen

The Double Oh Fool Guide to Tarot Mastery

Knowings from the Silence: Simple Wisdom for an Enlightened Life

Knowings from the Silence: Simple Wisdom for an Enlightened Life vol 2

Art is the Best Revenge: Poetic Deviance by Jim Larsen

www.foolspathtarot.com